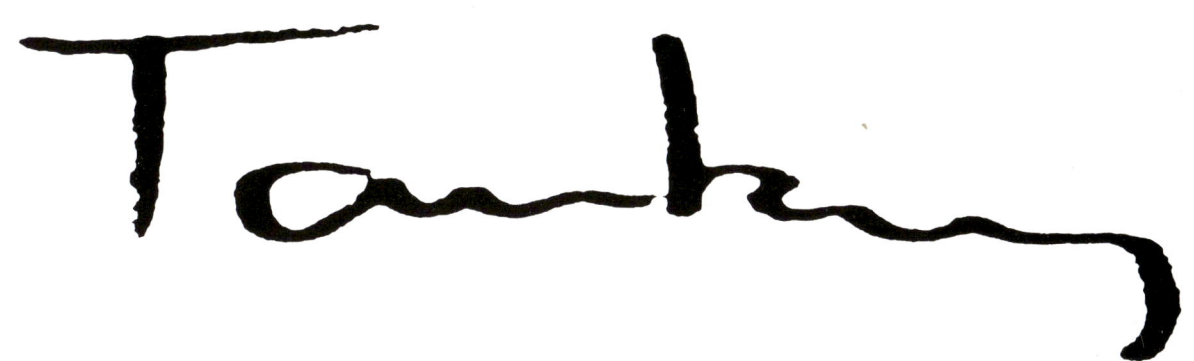

PROFILE OF AN ARTIST

TARKAY – PROFILE OF AN ARTIST

Copyright 1997 © CHEDWORTH PUBLISHING
ISBN # 1-883269-19-9

Printed by SunStorm/Fine Art Press
Ronkonkoma, NY
Printed in the USA

First Printing 10 9 8 7 6 5 4 3 2 1

PREFACE

Tarkay's own personal style of visual communication is evident in the body of work that he has created since the mid 1980s. Itzchak has grown artistically and creatively in the past two decades and has shared his work with the hundreds of thousands of his collectors and fans.

Tarkay–Profile of an Artist was conceived and created to share with the public a further insight into who the man is. The book explores this both through an in-depth interview, photographs of the artist at work and full color reproductions of his paintings, watercolors and recent serigraphs.

The pictorial section of the book is an interview conducted by Victor Forbes the editor of *SunStorm/Fine Art* magazine. Revealing in the subtleties of the artist's answers, this conversation with Tarkay is a form of "haiku", a verbal dance of joy and simplicity.

Tarkay–Profile of an Artist is the third volume on Tarkay, and certainly not the last. As we enter into the next millenium, history will most assuredly record his impact on the art world. As his publisher, I am proud to present this book as an offering to all those who have been touched by this renowned artist's work.

The book is dedicated, of course, to Itzchak Tarkay.

Leonard Panar
Chedworth Publishing
New York, 1997

ITZCHAK TARKAY

"The Hallowed Essence of Painting"

By VICTOR FORBES & RENÉE ST. JOHN

A modern master, very much alive and very much in the moment, Itzchak Tarkay draws upon the entire realm of art history in a body of work that is not only aesthetically agreeable and compositionally seductive, but a cultural phenomenon responsible for countless love letters, innumerable nights of passion and incalculable furtive glances—the very substance of visual poetry.

As a successor to the giants of art history in popularity, Tarkay's graceful personal iconography has generated over a hundred million dollars of sales in a decade during which the art market can be generously described as unstable. While the dollar value of art should, in a perfect world, have no bearing on the aesthetic value of creativity, Tarkay's ubiquitous acceptance by collectors must be noted. What chord does this man strike in the common thread that weaves through our universal consciousness? What note does he hit to get us howling in unison?

What it all boils down to is this: is the art worthy of our attention? Does it inspire? Does it have a light of its own? Or does it reflect a light far greater than that which can be discerned by our all too human eyes?

A man of great imagination and expressive gifts, with a special sensitivity and understanding of this life, Tarkay comprehends the duality inherent in man as one who should not only admire the beauty, but try to understand the sacred depths of this woman as well, thereby, perhaps, coming to terms with his own spirit.

If we can follow the path that Tarkay's woman takes inside of us, we will find a subtle mystery. It is here to explore if we will just scratch the surface. Let all that you hold onto pass for the moment, and Tarkay's woman will show you the way. What is the subject in the work of Tarkay? Is it the woman, or is it the shape of her? If we view his images with this thought in mind, the artwork will flow with answers. Not the logical kind of responses, but a primitive visual one. Modern art's abstracting of reality as we see it owes something to the art of Africa. Tarkay's work owes something to the early modernists as well. Though he abstracts his settings, he keeps them in line with the natural order of things. The gesture he carves speaks the visual language of nature itself. The shapes that he conjures seem gentle enough on the surface. Feel deeply as you explore Tarkay's world and another picture becomes evident—a picture of primitive power that etches itself into the memory. And in the memory, all that has gone before remains.

As the prolific and brilliant guitarist Jerry Garcia deemed each note he played to possess its own spirit, so must we consider each mark of Tarkay's to be imbued with a similar quality. There is life in each brush stroke, a tribute to one man's quest for peace and beauty. Overall, Tarkay's compositions appeal to our very hearts because they come from Tarkay's very heart. How could they not. As he says, "The love for painting runs in my blood." And nowhere is this love more evident than in the collection of work in which we see the coming of age of an undeniable talent. Though Tarkay prefers to see himself a few steps from the very pinnacle of the art world, if he is not at the height of his powers, he is certainly getting close. If you tell Tarkay he is at the zenith of his profession, he will smilingly tolerate such foolishness, and tell you if that were indeed the case, he would need to travel in two airplanes. The second one for his ego. As you will discover in this collection of his latest paintings and serigraphs, Tarkay as Maestro orchestrates masterpiece after masterpiece. We can only wonder where his next works will take us. In the studio, one on one with his vision, he shows us what he sees in a mode of expression all his own.

As heir to this mantle of artistic superstardom, with all the freedoms and responsibilities such a position entails, there is always a possibility an artist may rest upon his or her laurels. Not Tarkay. As is so clearly established in this volume, he demonstrates, by the sheer force and vibrancy of the art, not just a depth of color reminiscent of the Fauves and a compositional style also explored in the early days of Modernism, but a true understanding of human nature. In his endless panoramic view of the familiar, Tarkay explores new depths of emotion and sensuality. The universally acclaimed sumptuousness of Tarkay's color and line has now been transferred to his figures, giving extraordinary life and personality to *the natural woman,* as he so aptly describes her. This persona has become, especially in these incredible paintings of subtlety and magnitude, far greater than the sum of her parts.

While there was a time, earlier in his career, when it seemed that Tarkay was a somewhat casual observer, (if not a stranger) at his own party, in these works it is apparent that he has freed himself from any distance between creator and creation. What is so striking, and what assures Tarkay's position as an artist of the utmost importance, is that he has translated any emotional barrier into a flurry of emotional involvement. Whereas Lautrec, and in his earlier work, Tarkay, both seemed to assume the role of invisible spectator—perhaps voyeur—here now, Tarkay strips away any illusion of aloofness with a palate so sensual, so rife with love, that whosoever discovers this world cannot but be touched by the wisdom, knowledge and understanding, coupled with a healthy respect for life, that pervades his art.

Tarkay's roots as a painter take hold in the decisive years of modern art. The bright colors and flat patterns build on the paths forged by Matisse and the Fauves. Like Picasso, the sculptural grows stronger than the pictoral. He constructs a perspective and then takes it away. The paintings go through an abstract transformation, the perspective dissolves into colors and shapes, her face remains, and the world reconstructs around her. She is the natural woman—satisfied, calm, serene. With closed eyes, her blue eyelids open onto a different world. She is floating.

There is no solid earth in the paintings. Where solid earth is called for, the picture plane flattens to the surface of the canvas, bringing us into the here and now. Tarkay grabs the baton from the early emergence of modernism at the time when the Fauves made their stand. Yet he shies far away from comparisons, we just draw them here for the sake of scholarship and continuity. Tarkay's place in art history will be determined elsewehere. For the present, we have before us a collection of work by a man obsessed with his own vision. Beneath the seemingly simple concepts of "Natural Woman Living Life," Tarkay infuses his own power: the power of color, the power of line, the power of love. As Tarkay says: "In my case, it is funny. Before I came to be what is described as *famous*, I was in business. Slowly, slowly, I gave up everything from everything else and put all my love—my life—into the studio." Once this decision was made, a style was born. "If you watch my work, in many places there is abstraction—no drawing, no image—just color. That's how I began. The line is now, and has always been, very important. The composition brings everything together."

With the dawn of the 20th century and especially in paintings created in the time period 1905-1910, we see threads that have been picked up and sewn together by Tarkay. Threads laid bare by the Fauves, The German Colorists, and Picasso among others. Note Picasso's paintings of 1907-1909, for example, *Fruit Dish,* 1909. Tarkay uses similiar strategies: the way in which the fruits trail up trying to become spirals; the vase in Picasso's work, awkward, wrong and beautiful, like Tarkay's chairs. Tarkay takes hold of the perspective, molding the middle and foreground to his own liking. The alteration flows to the line of his gesture. He takes cues from Matisse, Lautrec, and the Fauves—but he is now. His work is more organic than that of the Cubists. His line works in harmony with nature.

The paintings evolve from a certain enigmatic shape, like the original form becoming a pear or an egg, reshaping itself into a spiral. With this shape, he constructs his world, and then it trails off, floating. The fullness of it, ripe, bountiful, like the woman herself. In Tarkay's words, "Everything we want and need can be found in a female form." Thus Tarkay's natural woman: the object of desire without responsibility or consequence. She is an icon. We see her in Matisse's *Odalisque* paintings of 1921-1923, and in *Woman in a Purple Coat,* 1937. Here we have the bountiful vase, the leaf shapes, the areas of color, the shapely woman in ripe repose. The foreground flattens to become the canvas as well. Of course, Tarkay is a modern painter, a painter of our times, with his own concerns. Is it any wonder with the state of the world as it is today, that Tarkay paints his image of a woman with her eyes closed? What does it take, in these times, to float in a world of your own? To go one on one with your dream? What does one need to take on a shape and embody a fundamental nature? Tarkay's work deals with these issues. In his paintings, Tarkay's abstract shapes become the subject as the subject becomes the shape. Her quiet mood everchanging, as the shape becomes itself.

What is the power that this shape holds? Tarkay builds his paintings with it. It is enigmatic. It is fundamental. It is more basic then ordinary logic and reason will allow. This is why it must be painted. It is a fluid shape, amorphous, seeking an identity. With eyes closed, his woman dreams herself into this shape. With a gesture, Tarkay's foliage blossoms it. His more abstract passages flatten to become this shape that is a building block of nature.

In defining this form, his colors are his own, full of Tarkay. His textures and structures melt and move—Tarkay. His women drift—Tarkay. Again, she is an icon. She is one with art history. She is blown here on the wings of time. She dreams her way into being. She's not unlike Cleopatra in a café. Did we not see her in the Sistine Chapel?

The freedom in these paintings says that Tarkay is not burdened by extraneous influences, in this way his is a spiritual art. Is She the pagan goddess at ease? Is She Kali Ma lounging amidst her creation, eyes closed like Sleeping Beauty? The flowers, fruit and leaves—offerings—shapes of color, nature's presence blossoming.

There is no school in this world where you could learn to paint like this. Probably, it's a hybrid of everything Tarkay has seen and done. Tarkay says that "As the paintings happen, you are involved so deeply in the work and what goes on around you and with you. It someday, someway develops, though always changing. But I don't feel the change, or think about it. It is coming, yet not under control…completely not under control."

Tarkay is concise, he is to the point, direct. He paints. He loves that. Oh, he loves a couple of artists, and would like to be remembered as one of the good ones. Yet, with this collection before you, Tarkay raises the stakes. He takes us to a place created by the cunning unity of mind, eye and hand. He loves, but doesn't deify his subject. Rather, he lets us do that. It's a very real goddess Tarkay illumines with his brushstroke. This is no craven image.

There is an ancient mystery in the work of Tarkay. That must be discovered for oneself. This is what Tarkay's paintings achieve. He brings to us this mystery for the advent of our coming millenium. His fertile female form is a timeless enigma. The poses that Tarkay's figures manifest are every bit as classical as *The Winged Victory* or *Venus de Milo.* Fifth century B.C.E. female figures, much like Tarkay's, can be seen on the Erechtheion in Athens. Tarkay dives deep into history, and brings up pearls for our times. The quality of his line is organic: the quality of his woman, his art, is magic.

Tarkay is truly a man at one with his gift. There is no barrier between his song and his substance. In the process of creation, it seems, Tarkay is able to reach inside and through some alchemy that melds the mystical with the mechanical, paint us a pure reproduction from his soul. In our process of creating this particular book, we have been blessed with the opportunity to glimpse the internal mechanisms of a genius at work. It's an over-used expression, absolutely, but in trying to find out what makes this man tick, we learn that Tarkay's brilliance is his ability to lovingly produce his inner vision without interference, in much the same way that Einstein discovered relativity or Beethoven brings forth a symphony. In the pages to follow, you have the opportunity to explore the work of Itzchak Tarkay, the mystery and the magic. We have used words to introduce you to the man and his tableau. By nature these words must fall short of the glory of his art. The paintings have their own tale to tell, linger with them, allow them to seduce you. They will. Each page is rich with his colors, every plate is your ticket to enjoy. A dialogue will unfold if you engage the work, page followed by luscious page, evolving into the kind of a story that only master paintings can convey. Become consumed by their subtleties. Become transfigured by their shapes. The power of art is unleashed upon us here, that hallowed essence of painting comes across.

Tarkay paints in the light of Israel. He doesn't talk about it as a Holy Land or make a big deal about spirituality, religion or politics. He is grateful for his health and concludes that "Life is good." His paintings, we noted, are as songs, even psalms. We would like to thank Tarkay for opening our eyes—the windows to our souls. As David, the King of his beloved Israel writes, "I will sing unto the Lord, because He has dealt bountifully with me." That stated, one question remains: Can there be a greater contribution to mankind?

"In the morning, after I wake up, I go into my studio and take my first coffee. I am in my studio around eight o'clock, sitting in my chair. If I have a good mood and know exactly what I want to do, it's ok. If not, I see myself at the easel, working—like hypnosis. You stand up from the chair and you don't feel it. You are near the easel, near the chair, and you are working. A normal day is ten hours. Seven days a week, except Yom Kippur. The work is really hard work."

—ITZCHAK TARKAY

50 Questions...

...Answered by Tarkay

1. When did you first realize you were coming into prominence as an artist?

It happened so fast.

2. Do you recall when you first began painting in the style that made you so popular?

About ten years ago, I started my general style that had been changed all the time—until now.

3. Who is that woman? Who are those women and how does she (or them) have such an importance to you that you are able to create such a large and impressive body of work revolving around her image?

Not a special woman, but a very natural one.

4. From where physically, and from where internally, do you get this seemingly never-ending stream of imagery?

It comes from the love to paint. That's the love that runs in my blood and is the center of my life.

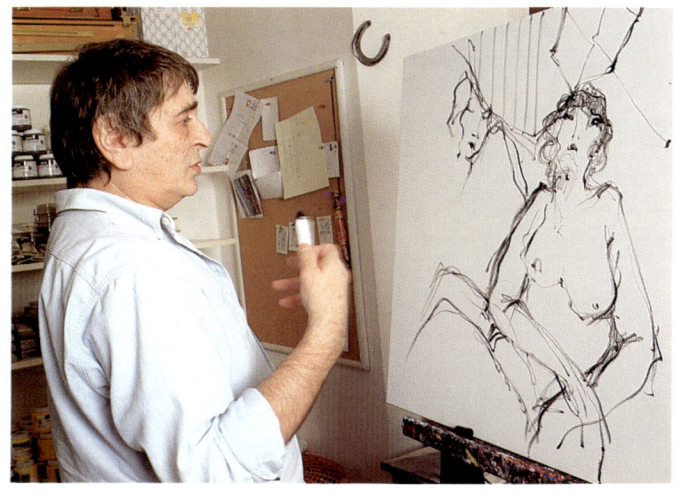

5. Who influenced you greatly—as an artist and as a man?

I don't think I was influenced by one person—maybe by many.

6. Could you imagine living as something other than an artist?

Yes, I could be someone else but I'd have to have the art by me.

7. Do you feel that you could have been a carpenter? A soldier? A poet? Anything other than an artist?

Who knows?

8. At what age did you first experience your need to paint and draw?

From childhood.

9. Were you encouraged as a child in this field?

No, I was not.

10. What obstacles have you had to overcome to get to where you are today?

Nothing.

11. What advice would you give others attempting such a journey?

Work, work and work!

12. How do you relax? Do you have spare time for hobbies or other activities?

Family and friends.

13. Do you go to many museum shows?

I enjoy visiting museums in Israel and abroad.

14. Have you ever taken a break from painting and tried another way to make a living?

Sometimes I do go on vacations with my family and friends, but sometimes, when I know that I'll want to paint, I take my things and paint.

15. Tell us about your creative process? How do you get these ideas? Are you always sketching? Traveling? Thinking about your next painting?

Sketching, yes. Traveling, yes. Thinking on my next painting, yes.

16. Did or does any other profession interest you?

No.

17. Is the process a complete mystery or do you have a set way to get yourself into the art?

No.

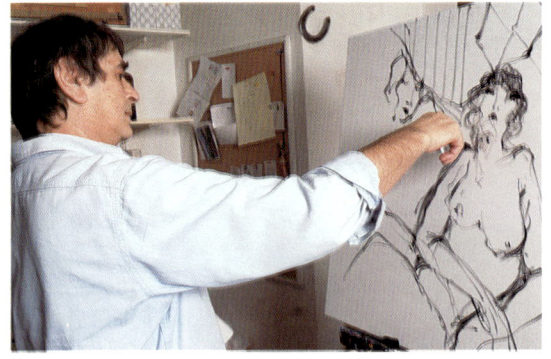

18. Where were you born? How was your childhood?

I was born in Yugoslavia in 1935 and had a normal childhood until the age of six. Then we started running for our lives in the concentration camps. When I was 13, I immigrated to Israel, stayed at a kibbutz and then the army. After completing my army duties, work and more work and more!

19. What about the environment in which you create is so important to you? Or can you produce your work virtually anywhere?

I paint anywhere I can, but I do love my studio as everything is set up for me.

20. Do you have some ideas for future works; different projects?

There are a lot of projects in progress right now.

21. Do you collect art or antiques?

Both.

22. Where do you work these days?

In my studio, in Tel-Aviv.

23. What kind of cuisine do you enjoy? What kind of wine do you drink? Do you listen to music when you paint?

I love eating meat and sushi, love good red wine and love listening to music when I paint.

24. How has your widespread acceptance and success affected your life?

Nothing has changed my life.

25. How would you like to be remembered as an artist?

As a good artist.

26. Are you getting to the point where you are going to be able to slow down? Or possibly change your artistic direction?

Yes.

27. Have you any thoughts on the state of art in the world today, and what meaning and value art has in everyday life?

Very confusing.

28. Why do you think, out of so many artists seeking success and popularity, that you have been so well received by the art collectors of the world?

I really don't know.

29. When did you begin to create limited editions?

About seven to eight years ago.

30. What is your favorite part of that process and how involved are you in print-making?

I am involved in the whole process and enjoy sketching on the prints the most.

31. Do you work on the screens, the plates, etc.?

I'm using this technique

32. How many prints by Tarkay are there out in the world?

I don't know.

33. Has your life and art been satisfying? Have you exceeded your expectations or do you wish to do more, bigger, better...

Satisfactory; and success is a mutual aim for all of us—so it is for me.

34. What about Israel is so important to you? So inspiring to your art and life?
It doesn't affect my work. It is my place and I can't even dream of changing it.

35. Where are your favorite places to paint? To sketch? To have quiet moments of creativity?

I like the most to paint in my studio, sketch and having quiet moments just about everywhere.

36. How do your surroundings interact with the creative process?

My surroundings (both landscapes and people) give me the urge to put my vision on canvas or any other material.

37. Are all your paintings thought out as sketches, or are you the kind of artist that can just stand at the easel and in a certain period of time have a painting?

Both

38. What media do you work in? What are your preferences?

I'm using many—acrylics, oils, watercolors. Those are changing to my mood.

I see myself at the easel working—like hypnosis.

39. Do you recall the day you went from being unknown to being famous?

It happened so fast, I haven't paid any attention to it.

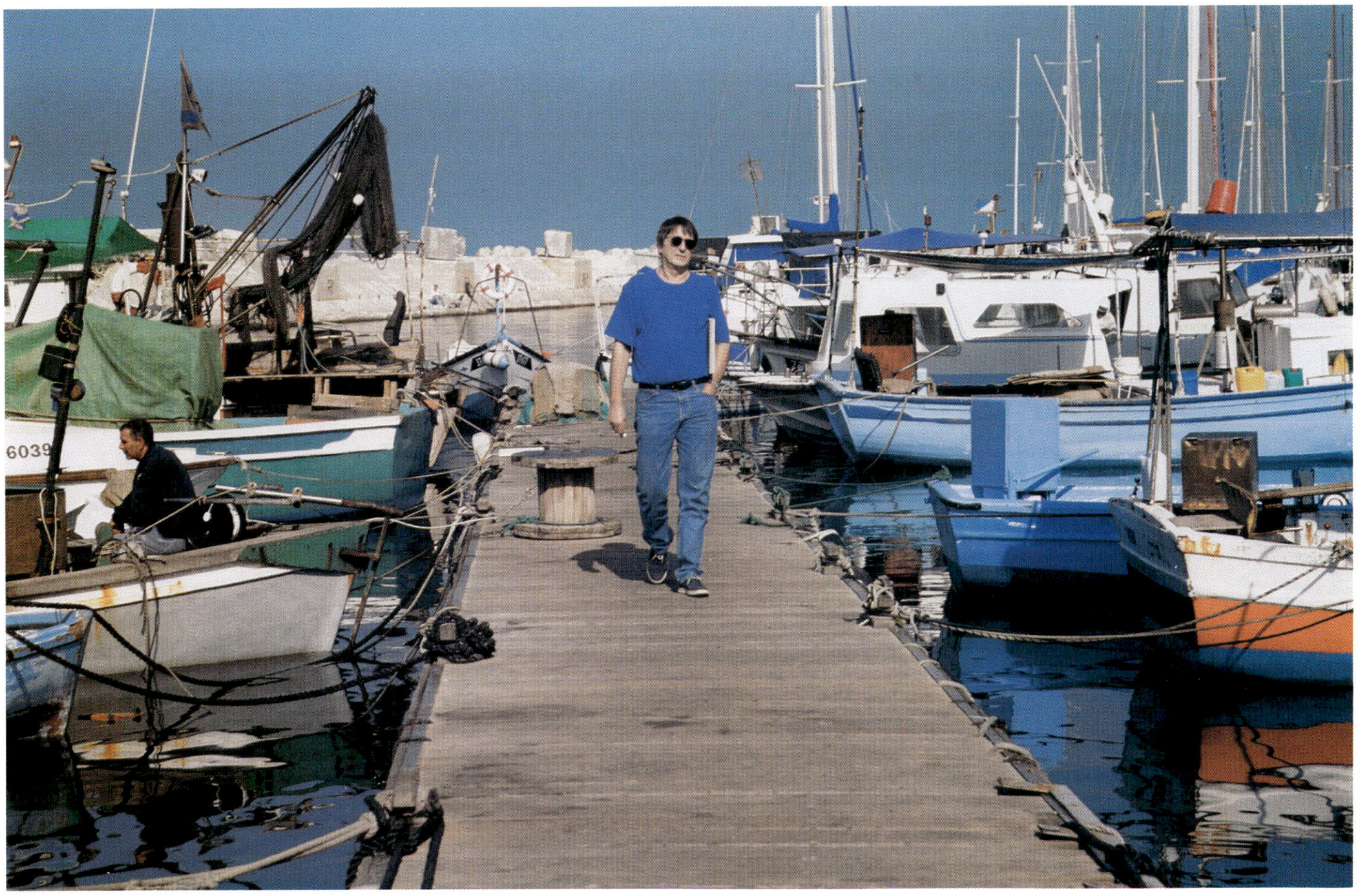
6039

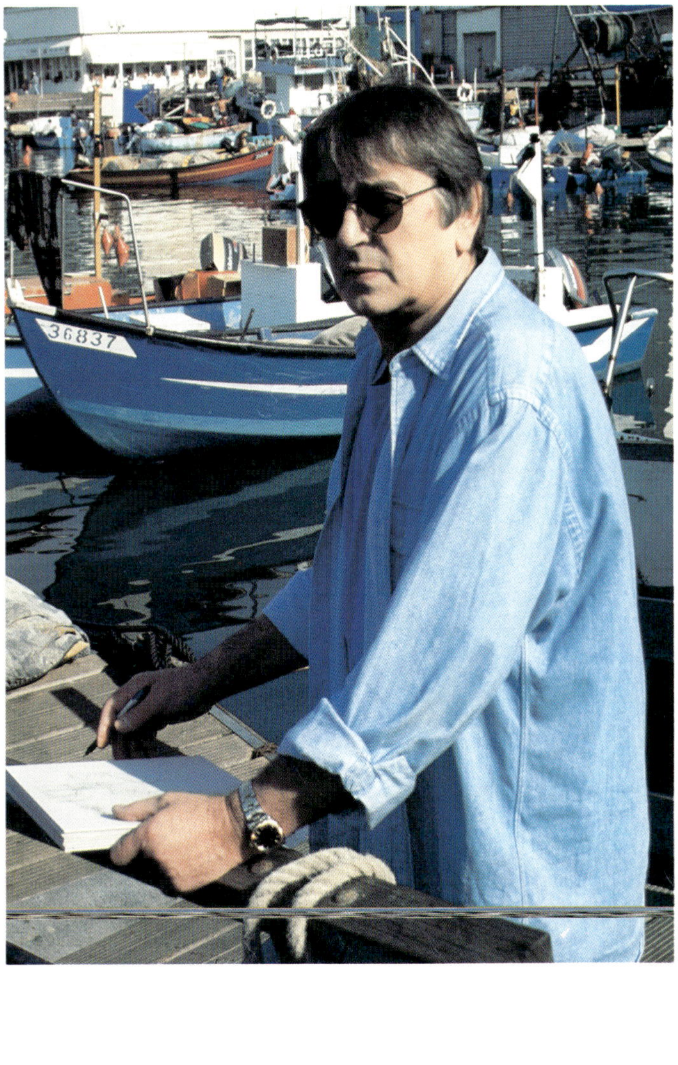
36837

40. How do you enjoy your fame? Your success? Does being successful give you strength to want to do more and better work? Or are you at the point where you can relax a little bit?

I enjoy my fame, though not enough due to to the fact that I am constantly working hard to get better and better all the time.

41. Are there any particular teachers or others who have had big or little influence on you and your art?

No.

42. What do you admire most
in the world today?

Health.

43. What would you change about the world
if you were able?

No more war—just Peace.

44. Do you think often of your Creator? And
in what sense do you compare
your acts of creation to those of
the Creator of the Universe?

It's too big for an answer.

45. Have you been blessed with any special knowledge, or special insight that opens up these beautiful artistic visions for you? Is this a mystical process that you are still figuring out?

I am still figuring it out.

46. Do you have to be a special kind of person to be an artist, or does it really matter?

No.

47. You seem to be drawn to the sea. Does being near the water inspire your work, or inspire you to work?

No.

48. What do you view as your major accomplishments in this life—as an artist and as a person?

It's a question that doesn't interfere with me.

49. What if any, are your major disappointments?

I do not expect much so I don't have too many disappointments.

50. Have you any conclusions (about anything) you would like to share with us?

Life is good.

SUZANNE
40" x 50"
Acrylic on Canvas

GHISLAINE
29⅛" x 31½"
Serigraph, Edition of 350

SIMONE
29 ⅝" x 31½"
Serigraph, Edition of 350

CELESTE
14" x 14"
Serigraph, Edition of 350

49

WAITING
24" x 32"
Acrylic on Canvas

51

CIRCUS MAXIMUS
40" x 50"
Acrylic on Canvas

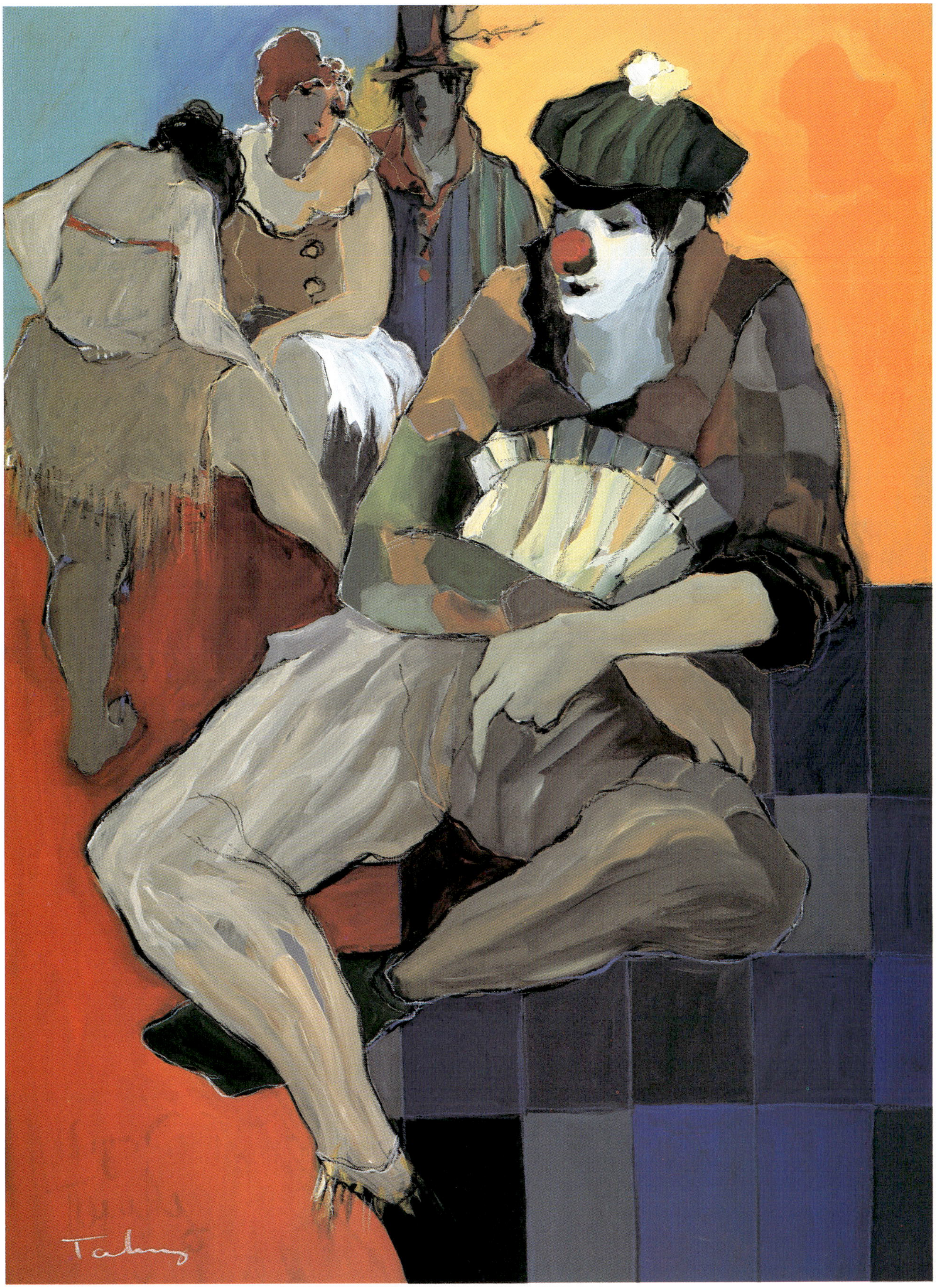
Tarkay

TIRED AT TEA
55" x 23½"
Acrylic on Canvas

AFTER THE PARTY
32¼" x 40¼"
Acrylic on Canvas

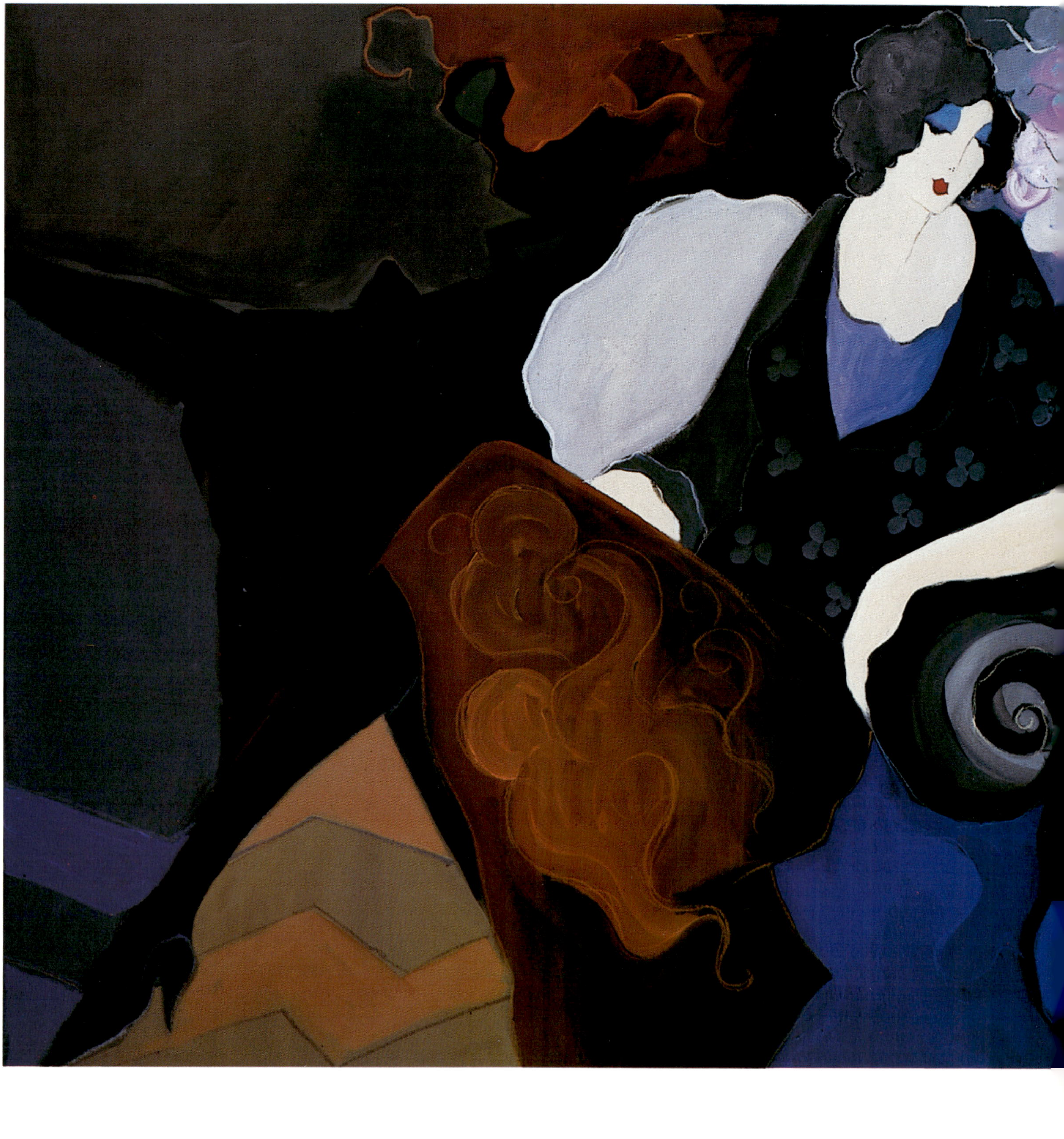

PRIVATE CHAT
21¼" x 42½"
Serigraph, Edition of 350

JANE
28" x 32"
Arcylic on Canvas

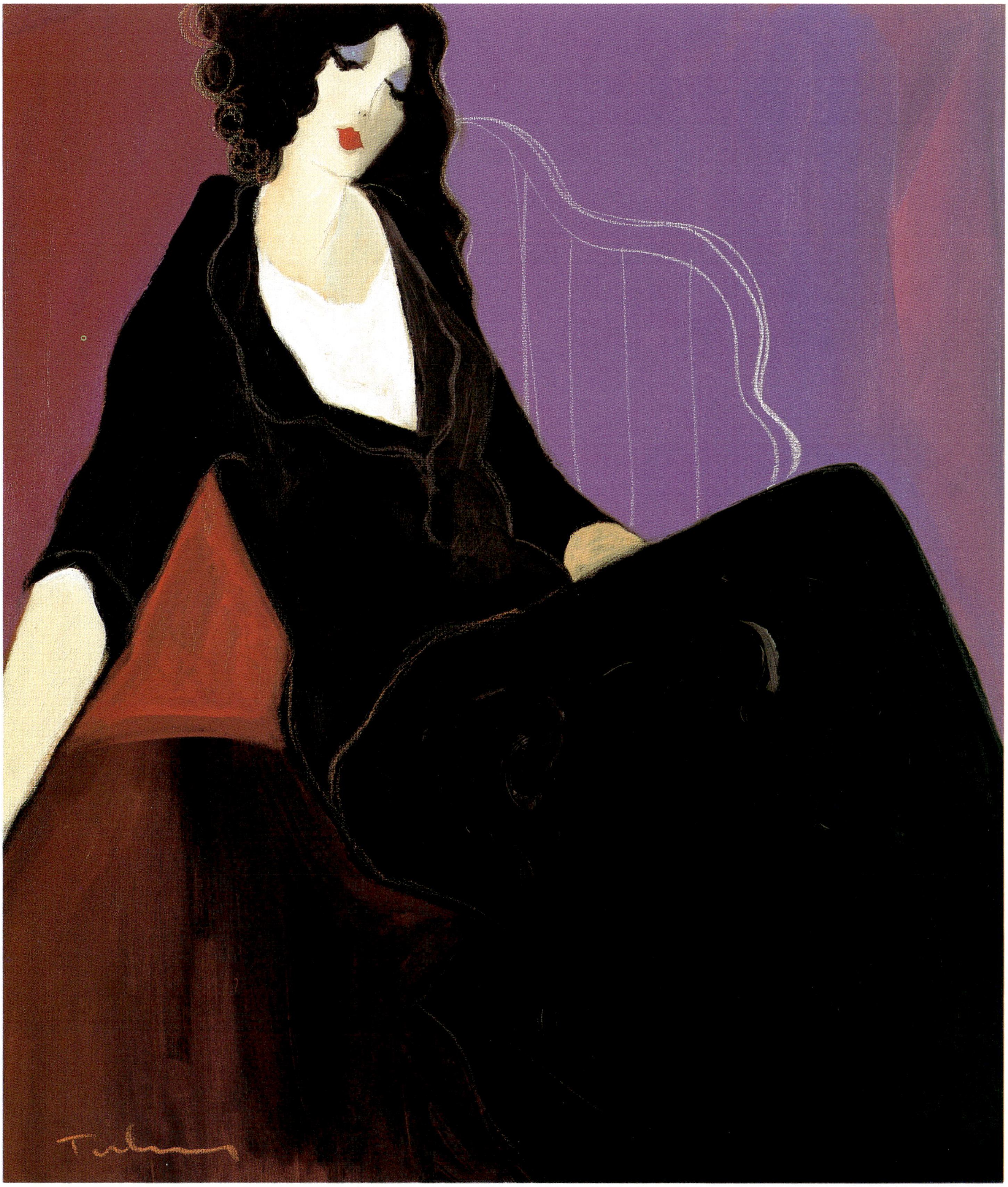

KARLY
55" x 23½"
Acrylic on Canvas

ESTELLE
45½" x 28½"
Acrylic on Canvas

LES AMIS TOUJOURS
24" x 32"
Acrylic on Canvas

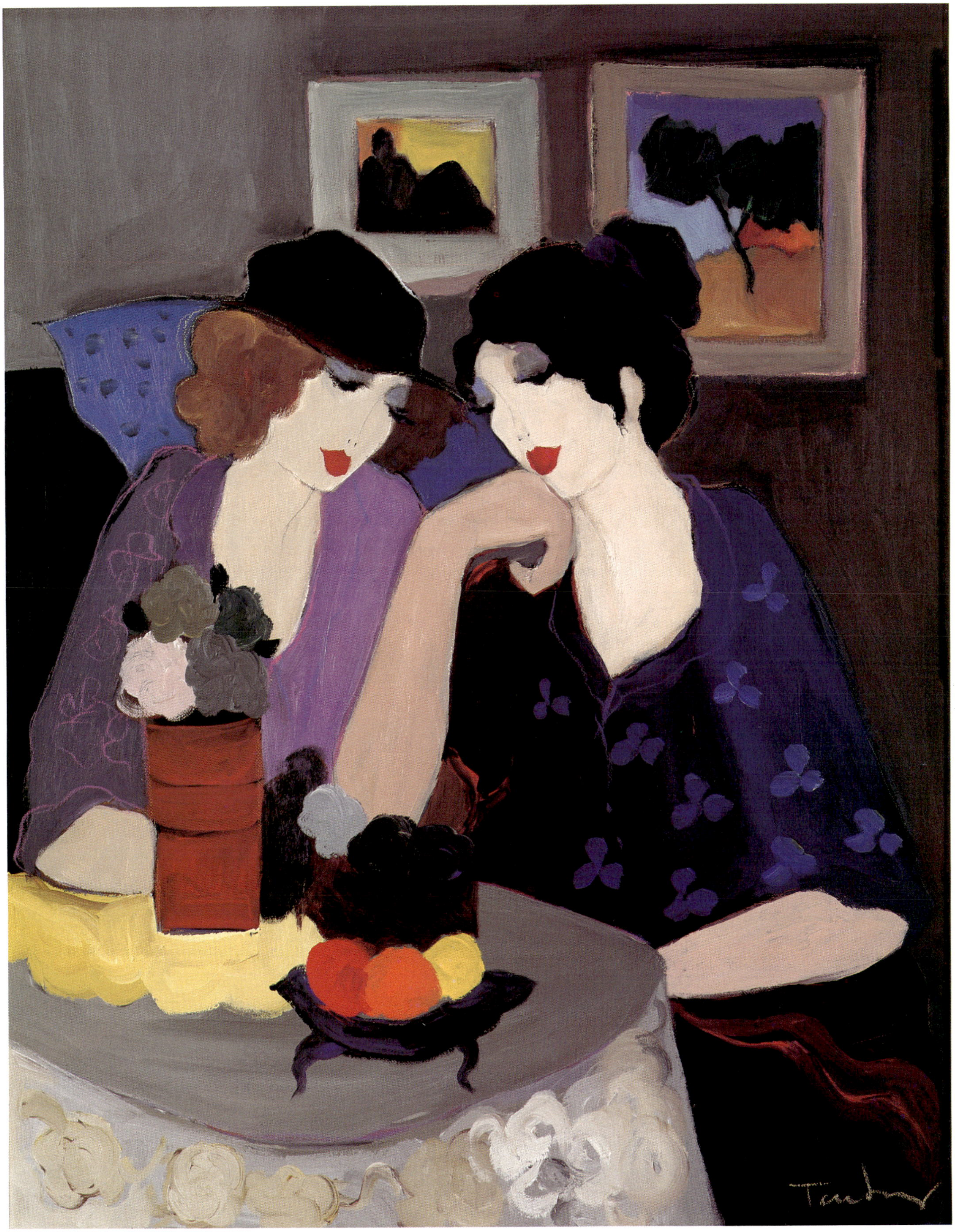

STANDING NUDE
24" x 32"
Acrylic on Canvas

65

NICOLE
29¼" x 36"
Serigraph, Edition of 350

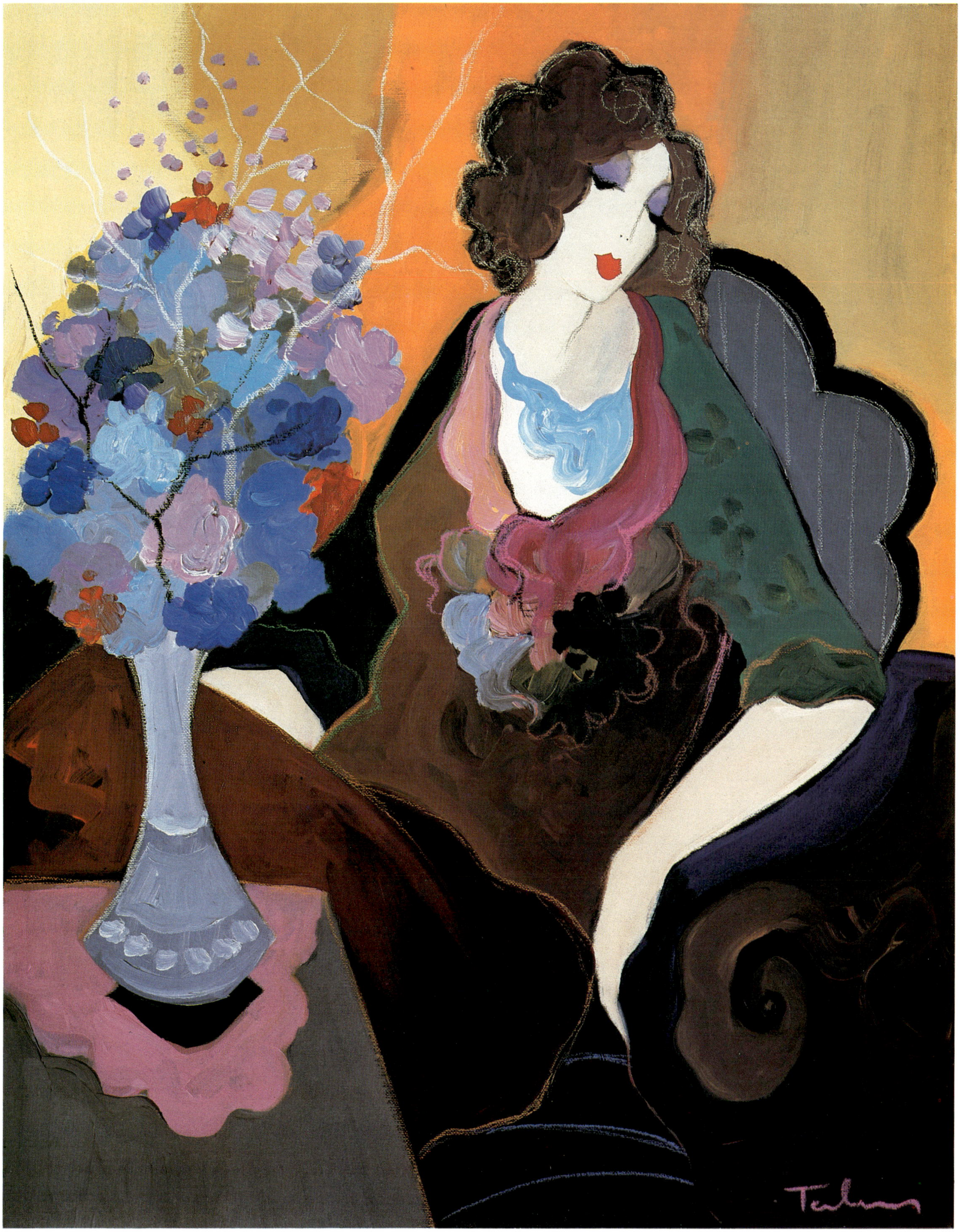

JEANINE
32¼" x 26⅜"
Serigraph, Edition of 350

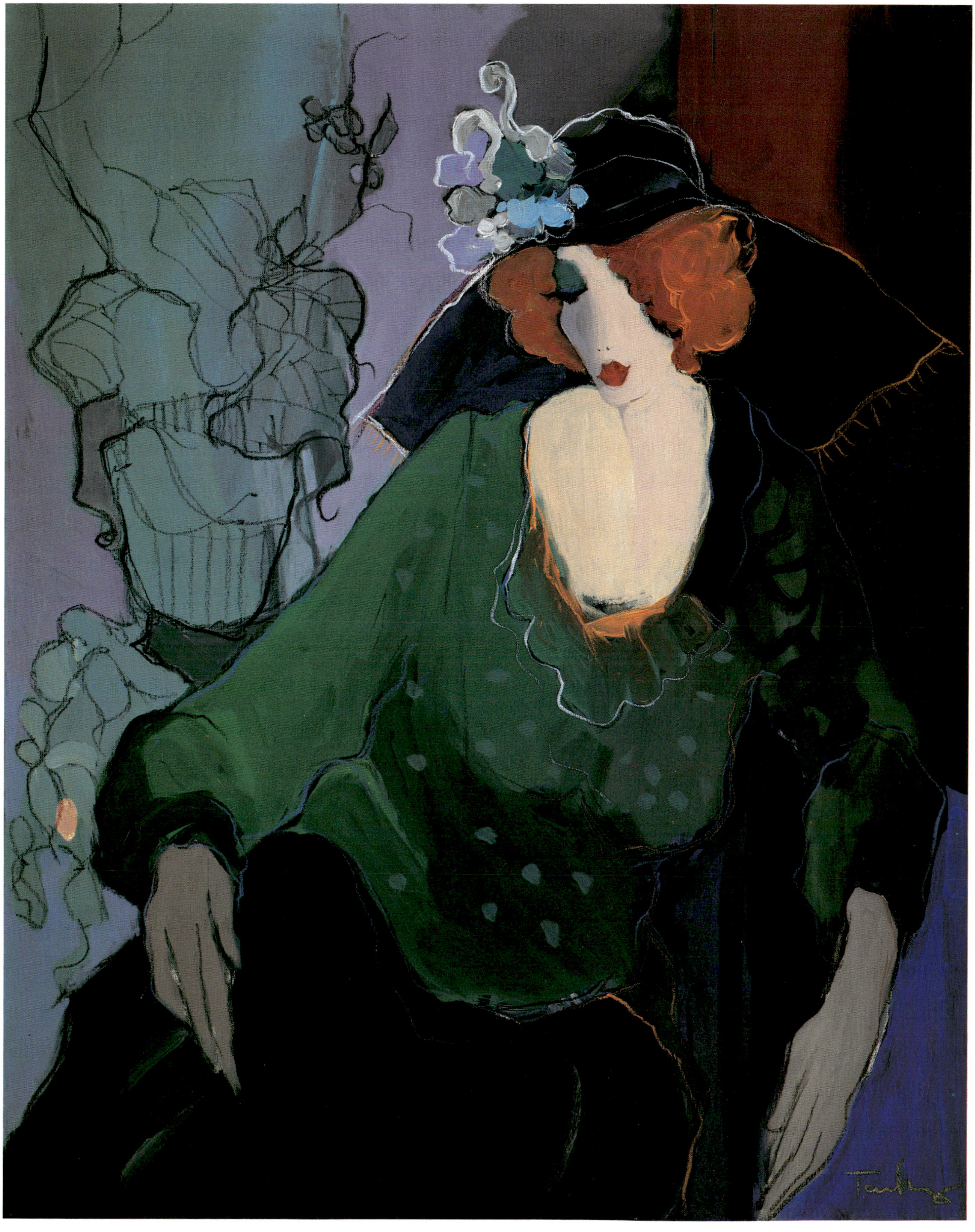

TABITHA
40¼" x 32¼"
Acrylic on Canvas

WANDA
25 ¾" x 21 ¼"
Acrylic on Canvas

71

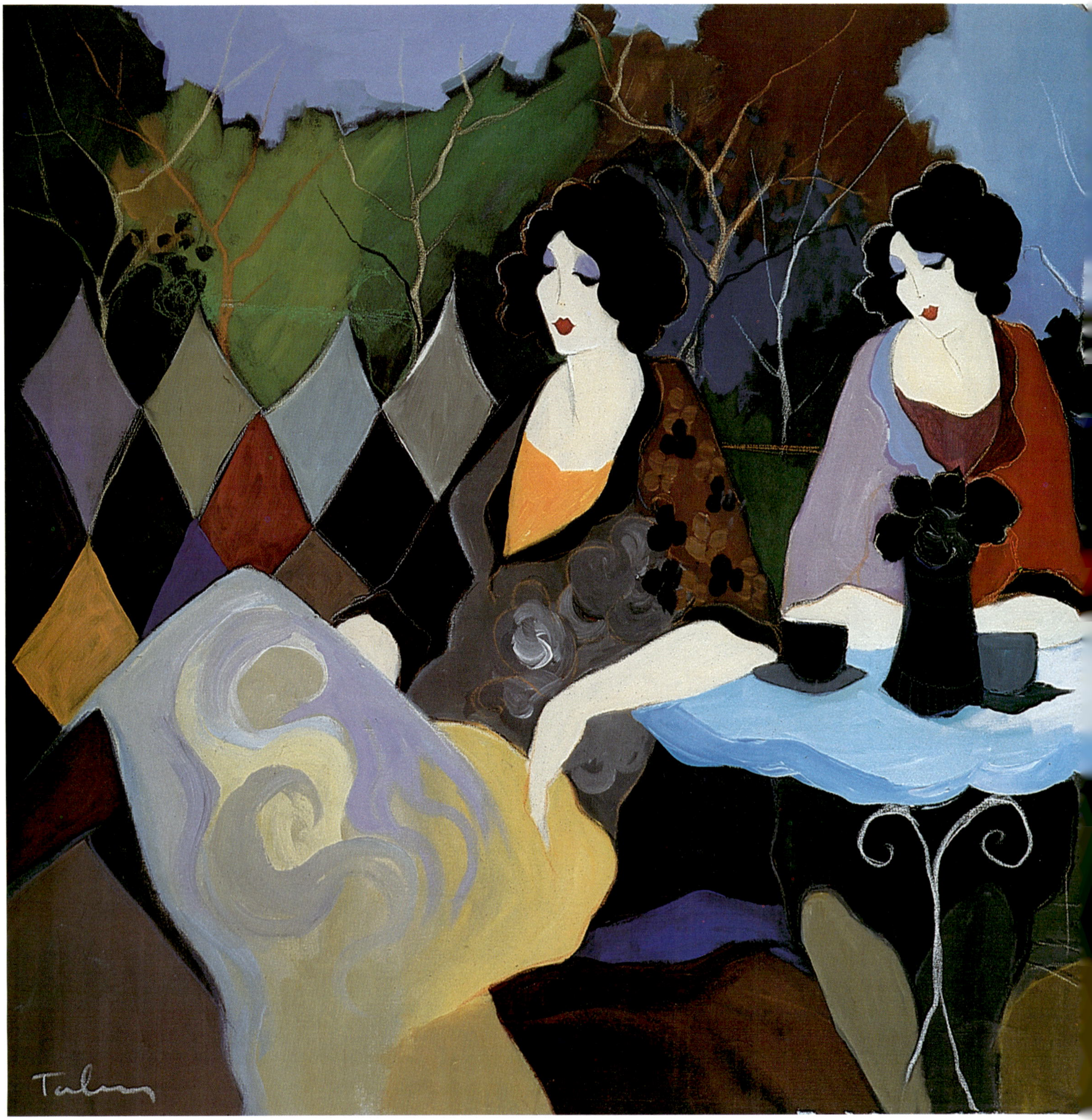
Tarkay

AFTERNOON LUNCHEON
14³⁄₁₆" x 28⅜"
Serigraph, Edition of 350

73

ELOISA
28" x 32"
Arcylic on Canvas

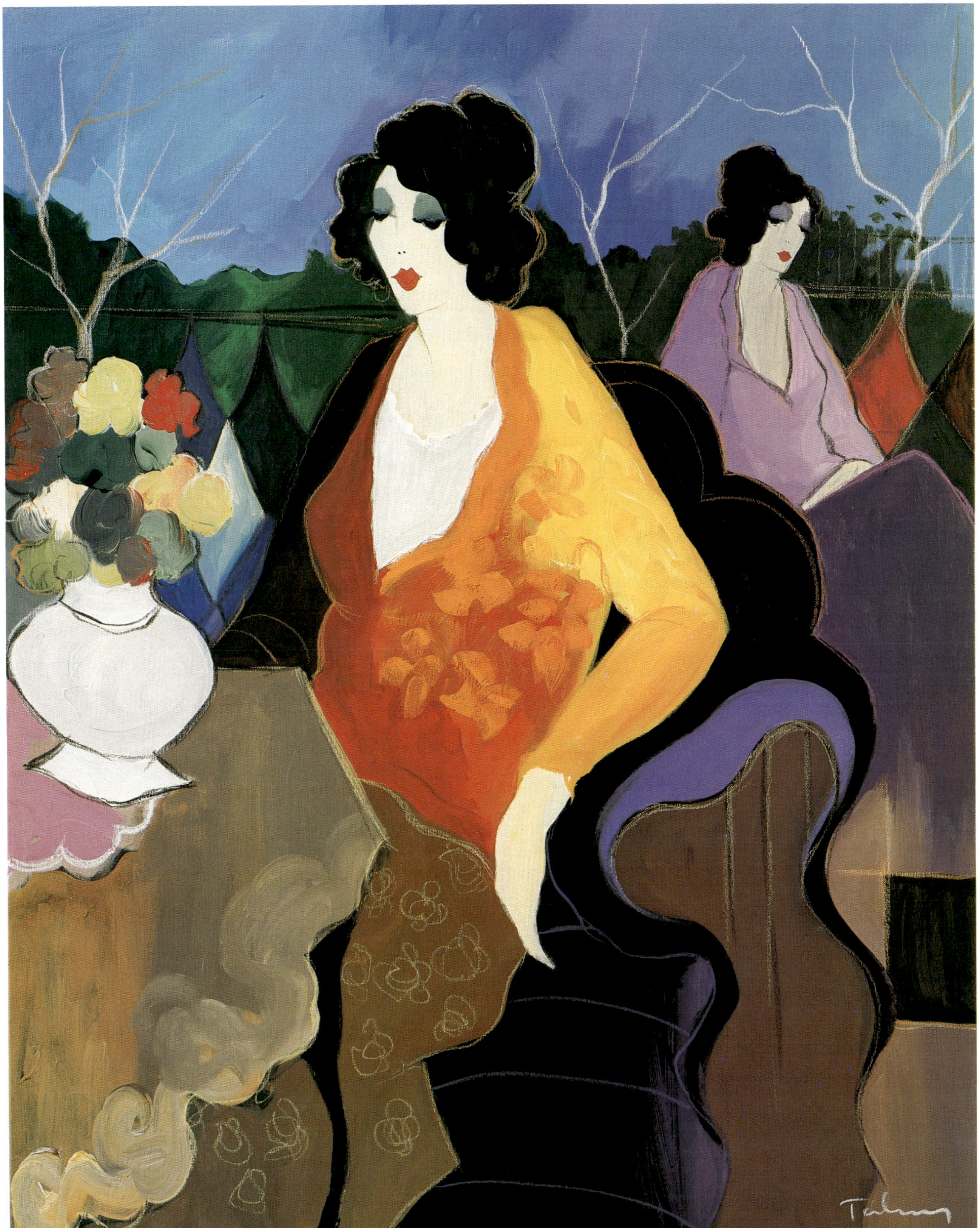

CARLA
31⅞" x 27¾"
Acrylic on Canvas

77

APRES MIDI
32" x 40"
Acrylic on Canvas

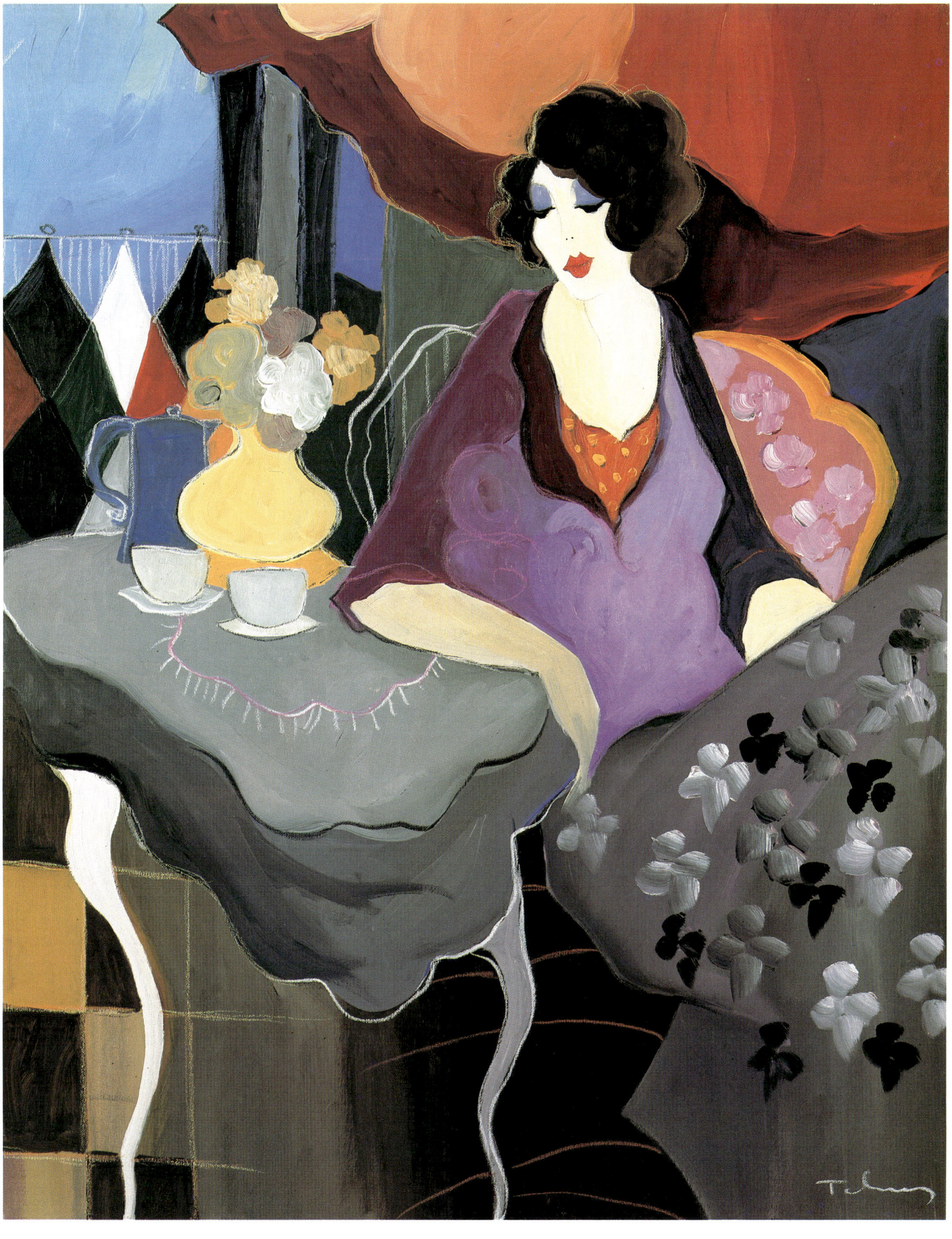

CHERYL
40" x 50"
Acrylic on Canvas

LADIES STANDING
18⅛" x 22⁷⁄₁₆"
Serigraph, Edition of 350

TEA NEAR THE WATER
33" x 40½"
Acrylic on Canvas

JEANNE
29⅝" x 30"
Serigraph, Edition of 350

83

PHEOBE
32" 40"
Acrylic on Canvas

SOLITUDE III
11⅞" x 11⅞"
Serigraph, Edition of 350

85

Pages 88-89:
ELEGANCE TOUJOUR
30" x 60"
Acrylic on Canvas

CHARLOTTE SEATED
9⅞" x 11⅞"
Serigraph, Edition of 350

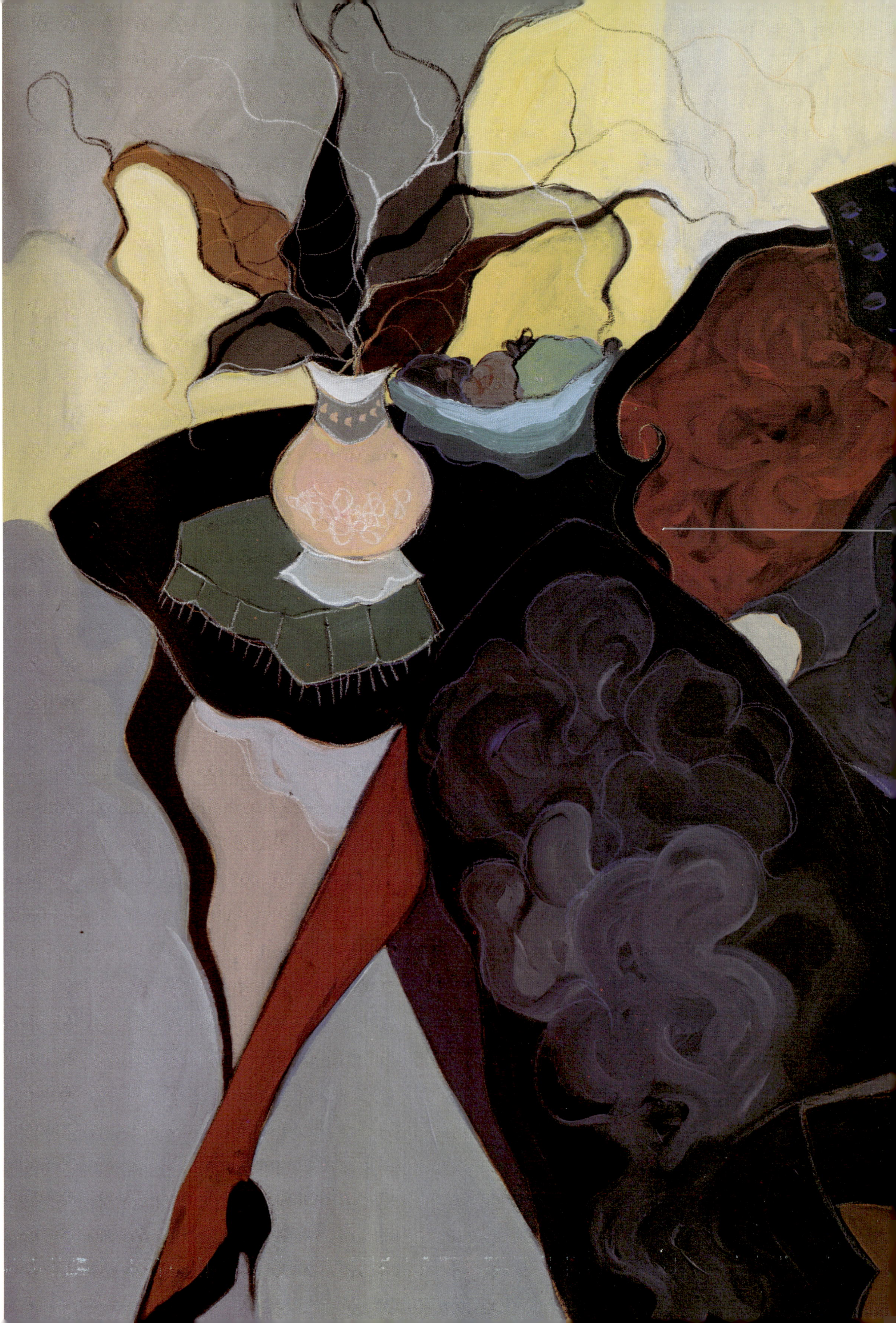

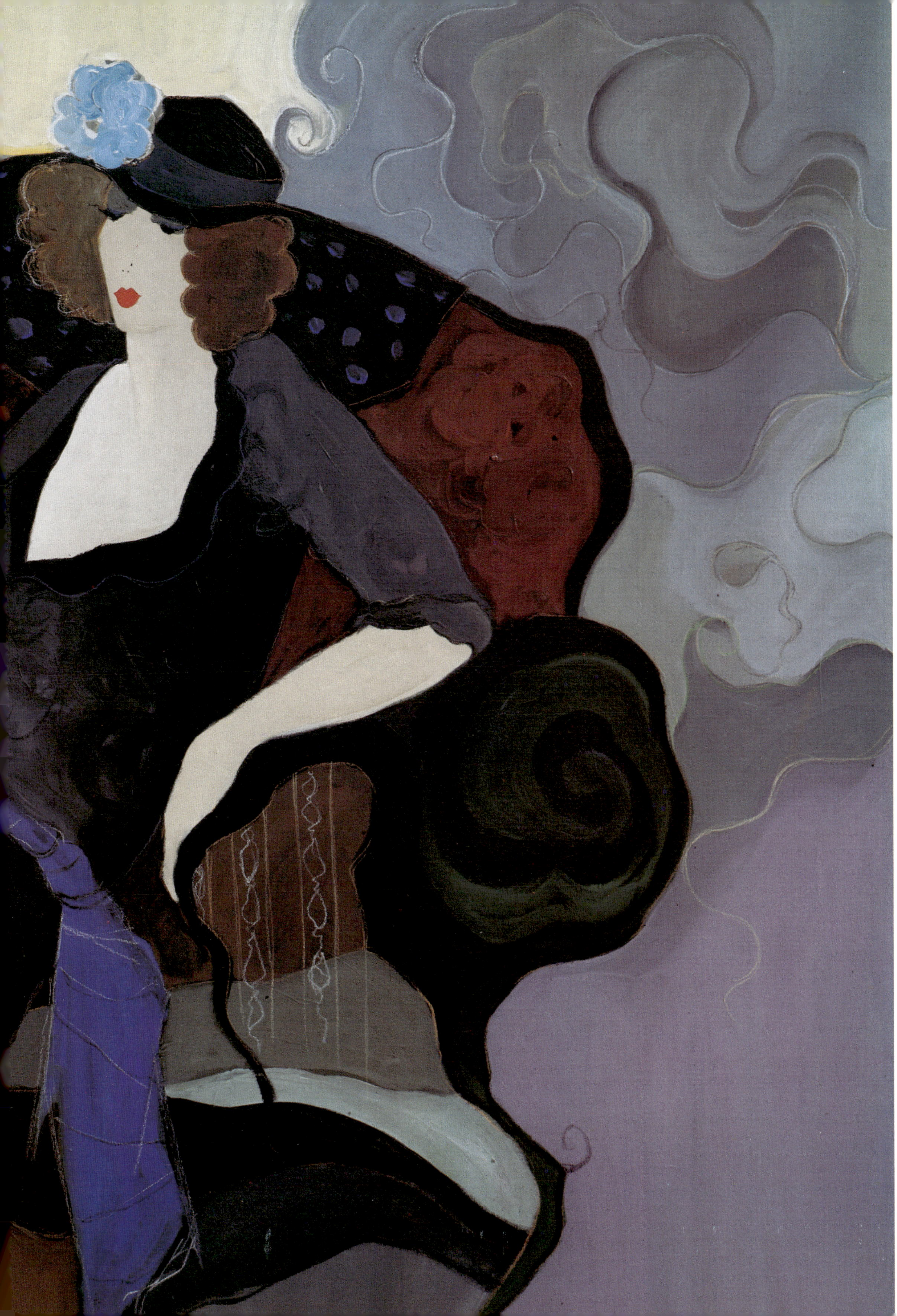

LAZY TIME
55" x 23¾"
Acrylic on Canvas

SISTERS
11⅞" x 11⅞"
Serigraph, Edition of 350

HANNA
29 ¾" x 29 ¾"
Acrylic on Canvas

FRENCHWOMAN
30" x 30"
Acrylic on Canvas

BECKY & DONNA
45" x 57½"
Acrylic on Canvas

WINNIE
40" x 40"
Acrylic on Canvas

BARBARA
28" x 32"
Acrylic on Canvas

DIANE FORGETS
38½" x 51"
Acrylic on Canvas

SANDY AND TAMMY
53¼" x 28"
Acrylic on Canvas

FOUR AFTER THE PARTY
45" x 57½"
Acrylic on Canvas

SAMEDI SOIR
24" x 24"
Serigraph, Edition of 350

103

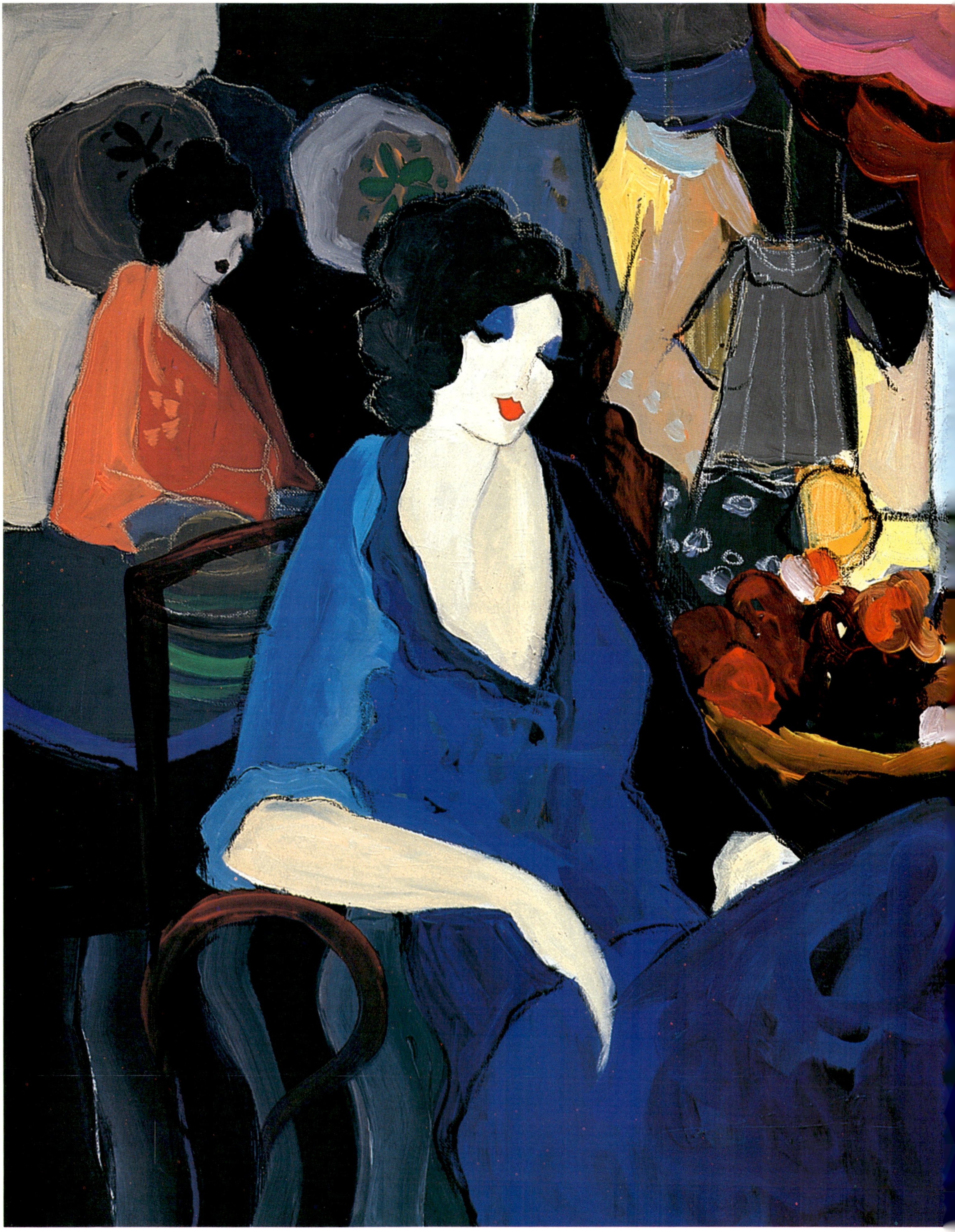

WOMEN AT MARKET
29" x 46"
Acrylic on Canvas

EVENING TALK
39½" x 39½"
Acrylic on Canvas

CHANGING ALEX
40" x 50"
Acrylic on Canvas

BEATRICE
21½" x 18"
Acrylic on Canvas

DIANE REMEMBERS
38¼" x 51¼"
Acrylic on Canvas

SENSUALITY
40" x 50"
Acrylic on Canvas

LIZA
9 ⅞" x 11 ⅞"
Serigraph, Edition of 350

SPECIAL NITE
18 ⅛" x 20 ⅞"
Serigraph, Edition of 350

KATHERINE
14" x 14"
Serigraph, Edition of 350

115

BARBARA & GAYLE
40¼" x 32¼"
Acrylic on Canvas

ERICA IN HAT
9 ⅞" x 11 ⅞"
Serigraph, Edition of 350

DEBBIE
21½" x 18"
Acrylic on Canvas

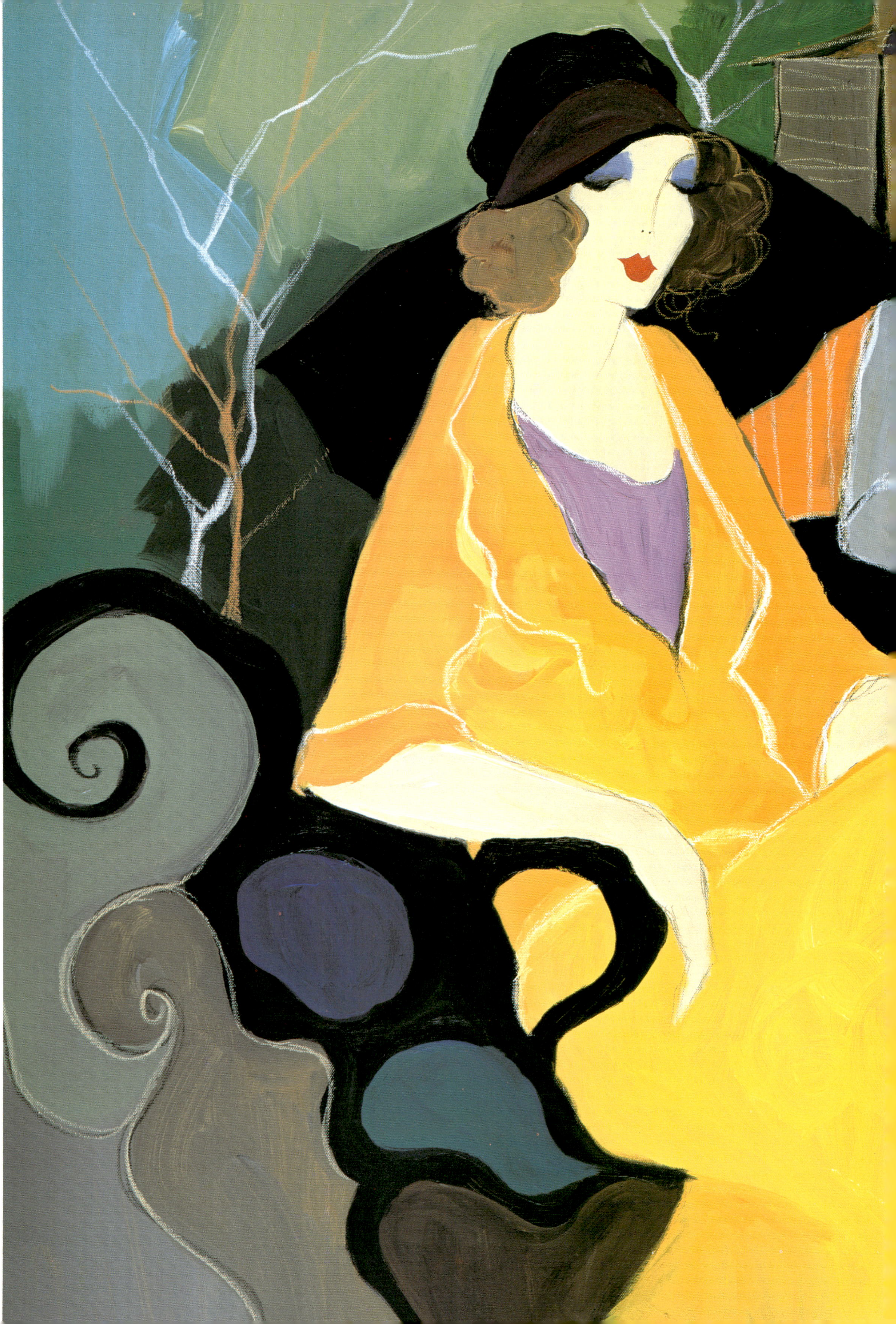

121

Preceding Pages

POLITE CONVERSATION
30" x 40"
Acrylic on Canvas

NELLIE
40¼" x 40"
Acrylic on Canvas

GIA
29" x 23½"
Acrylic on Canvas

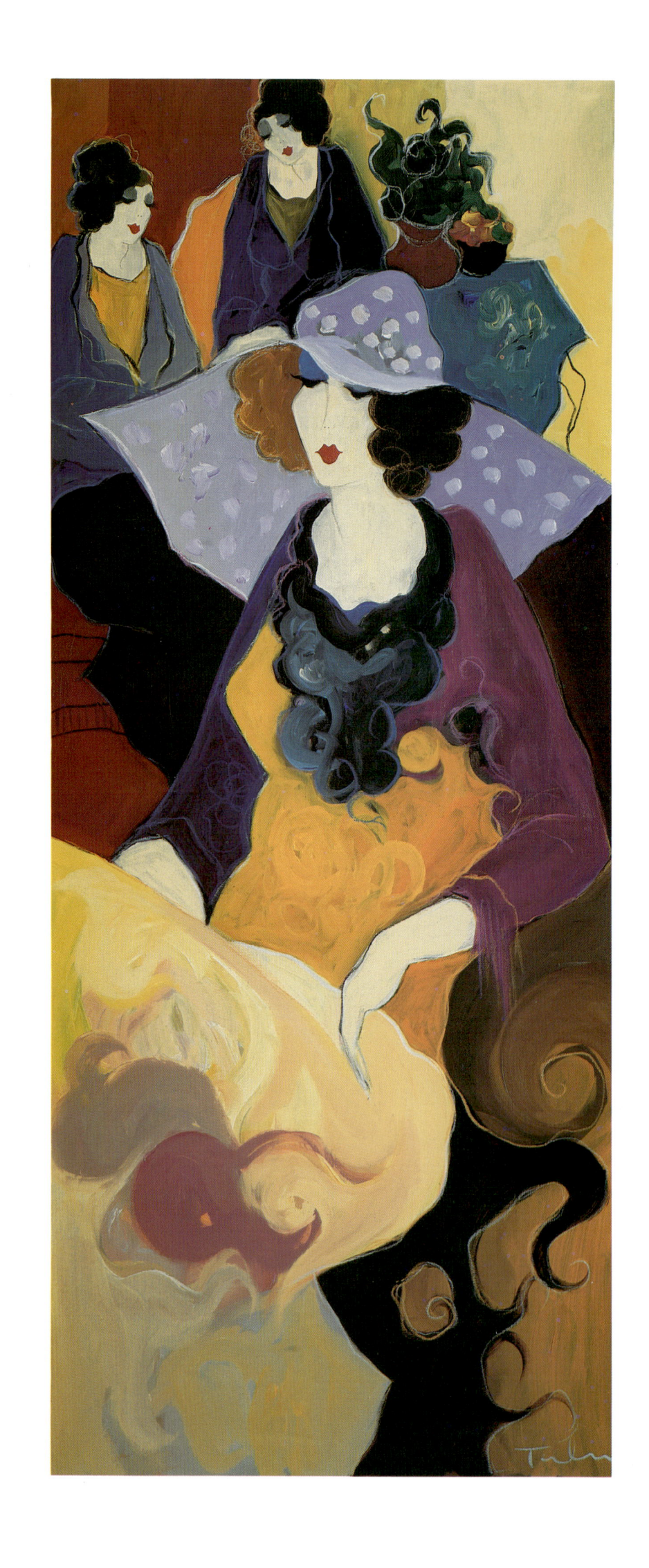

LAVENDER HAT
18⅛" x 42½"
Serigraph, Edition of 350

LADY IN BIG RED HAT
39 ⅞" x 40"
Serigraph, Edition of 350

126

LADIES TEA
14 3/16" x 28 3/8"
Serigraph, Edition of 350

EVENING RESPITE
18⅛" x 42½"
Serigraph, Edition of 350

THREE FOR DESSERT
38¼" x 51¼"
Acrylic on Canvas

THREE AT NOON
55" x 23¾"
Acrylic on Canvas

LOVELINES
38 3/16" x 38 3/16"
Serigraph, Edition of 350

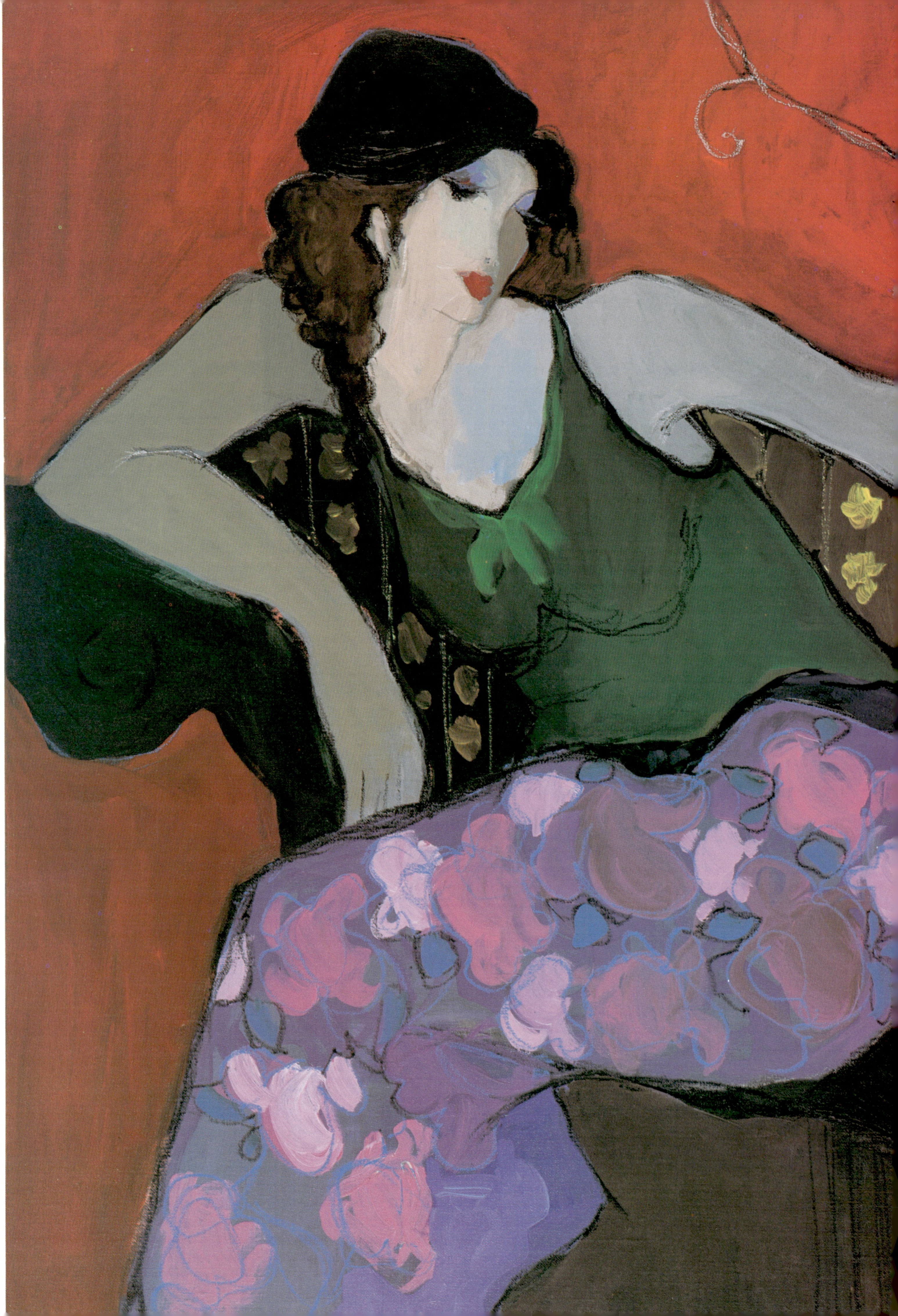

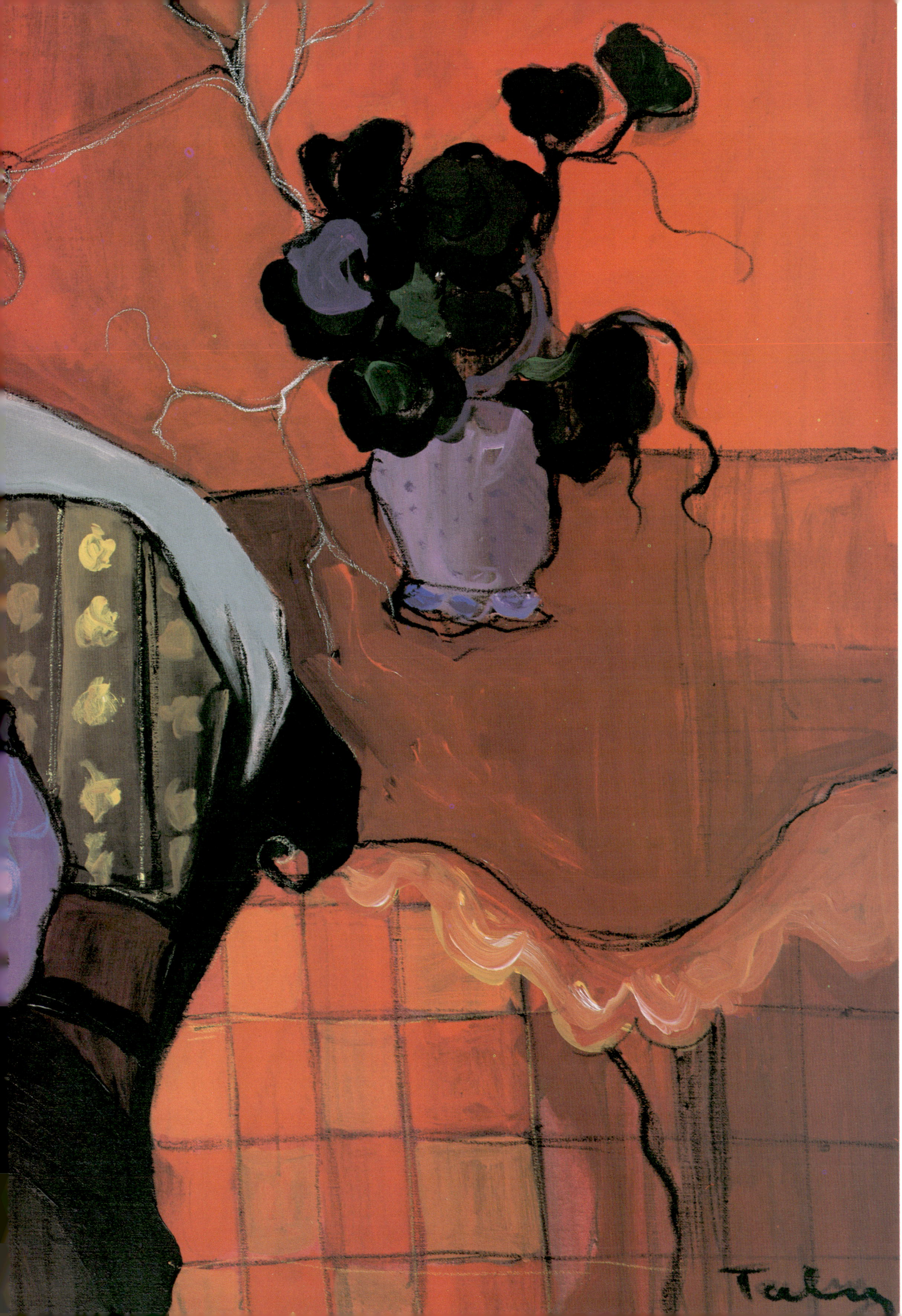

Watercolors

Preceding Pages:
MODEL POSING
40" x 50"
Serigraph, Edition of 350

UNTITLED
11½" x 15¾"
Serigraph, Edition of 350

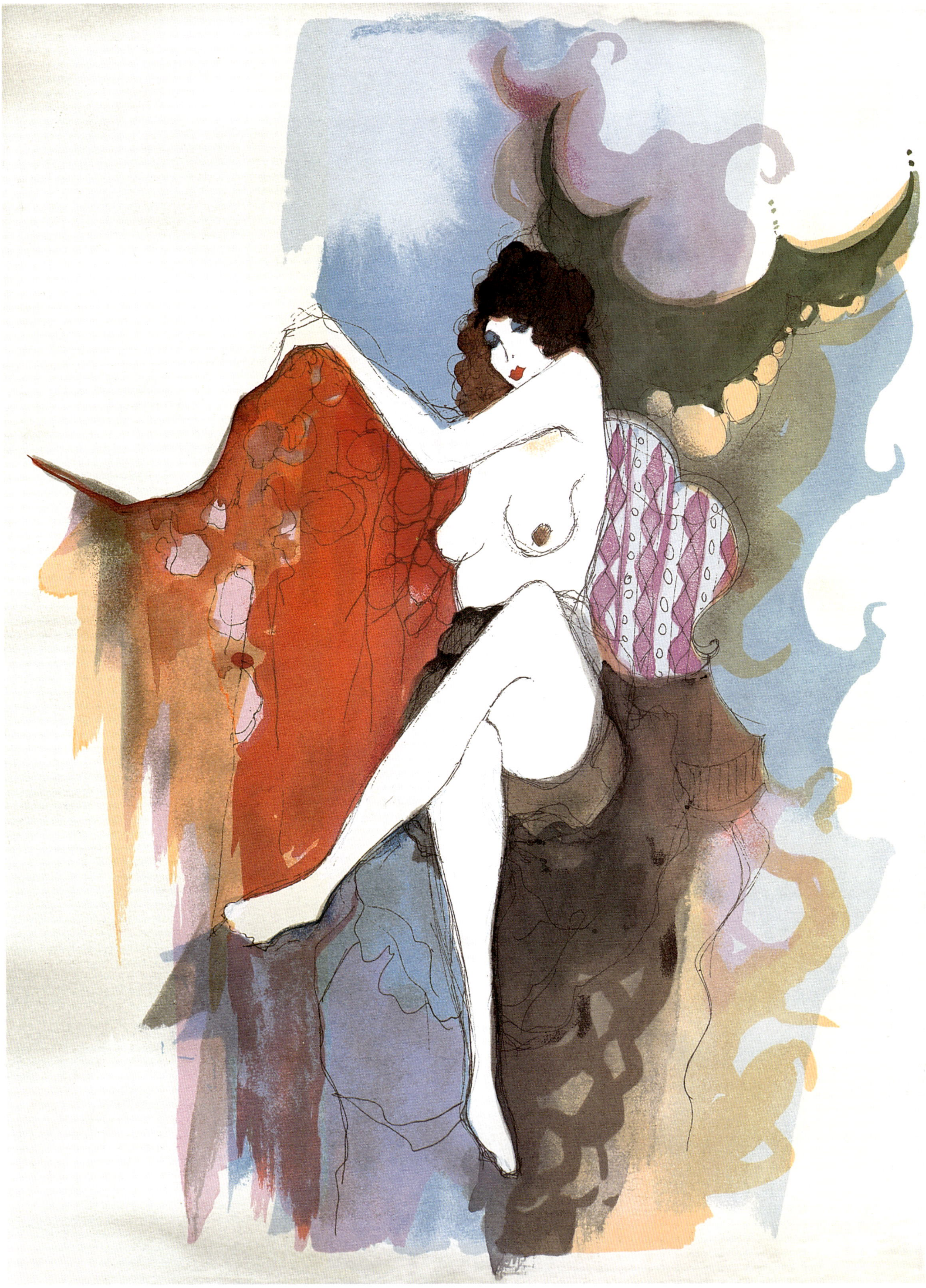

UNTITLED
11½" x 15¾"
Serigraph, Edition of 350

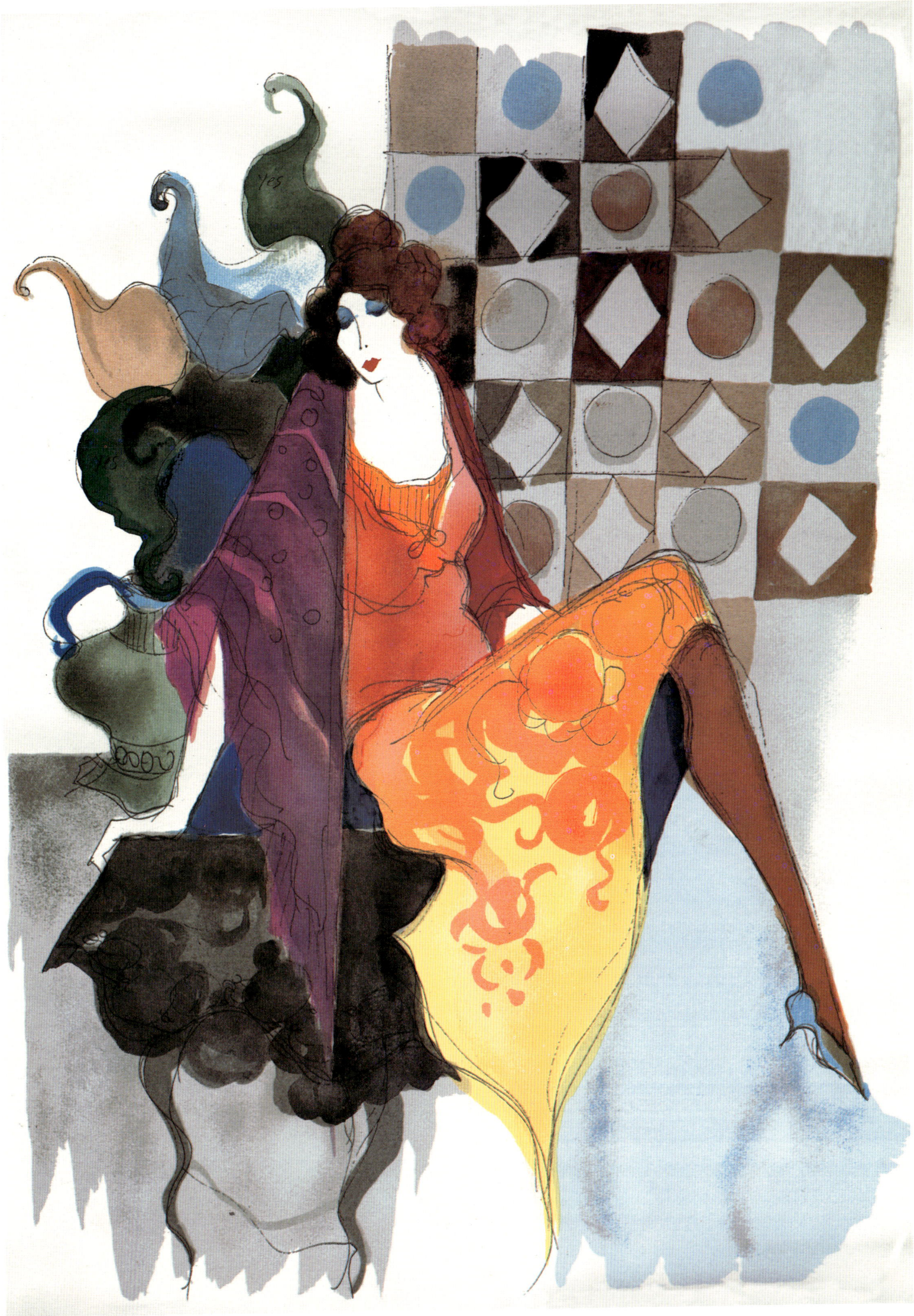

UNTITLED
11½" x 15¾"
Serigraph, Edition of 350

139

UNTITLED
11½" x 15¾"
Serigraph, Edition of 350

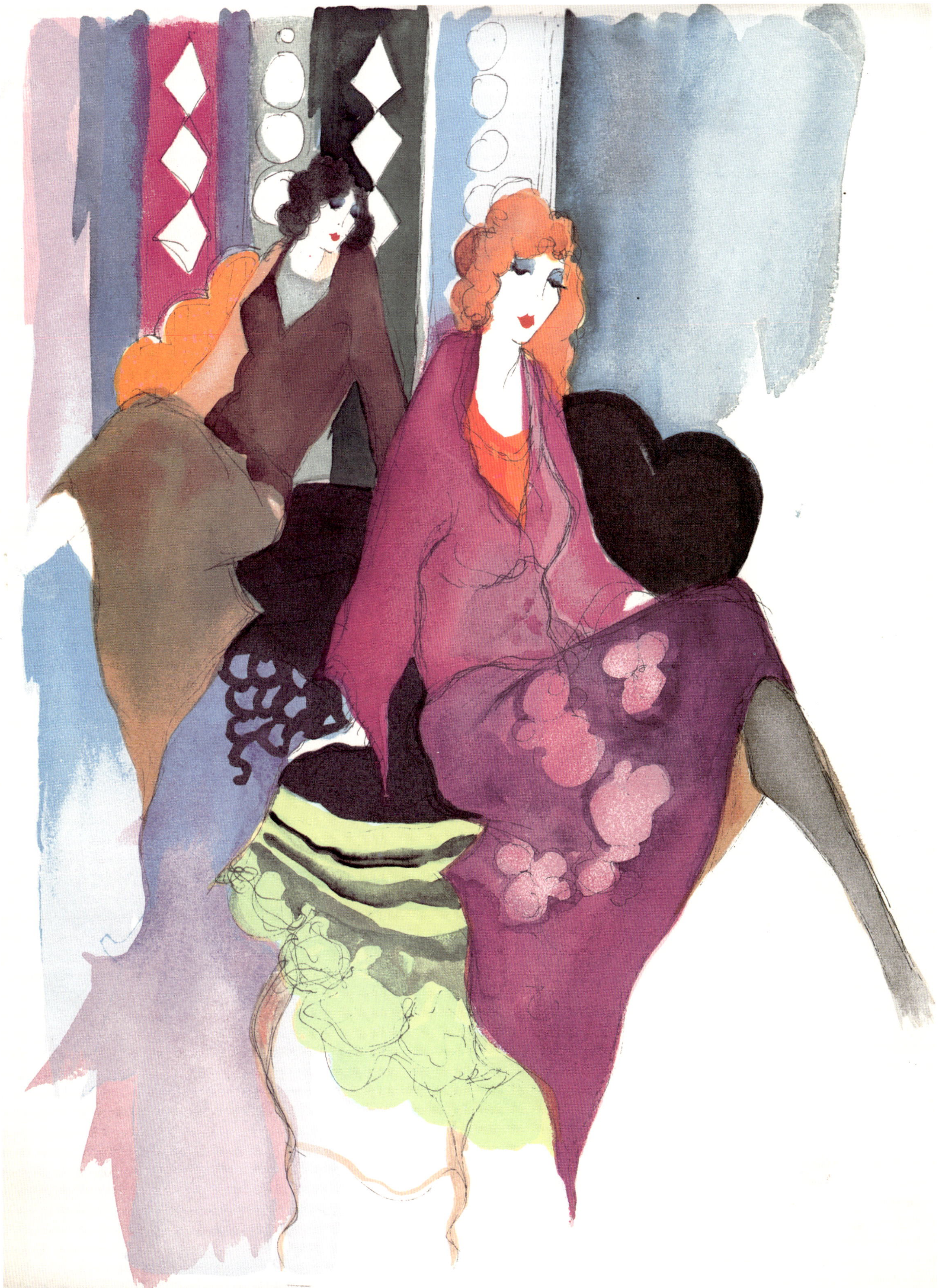

UNTITLED
11½" x 15¾"
Serigraph, Edition of 350

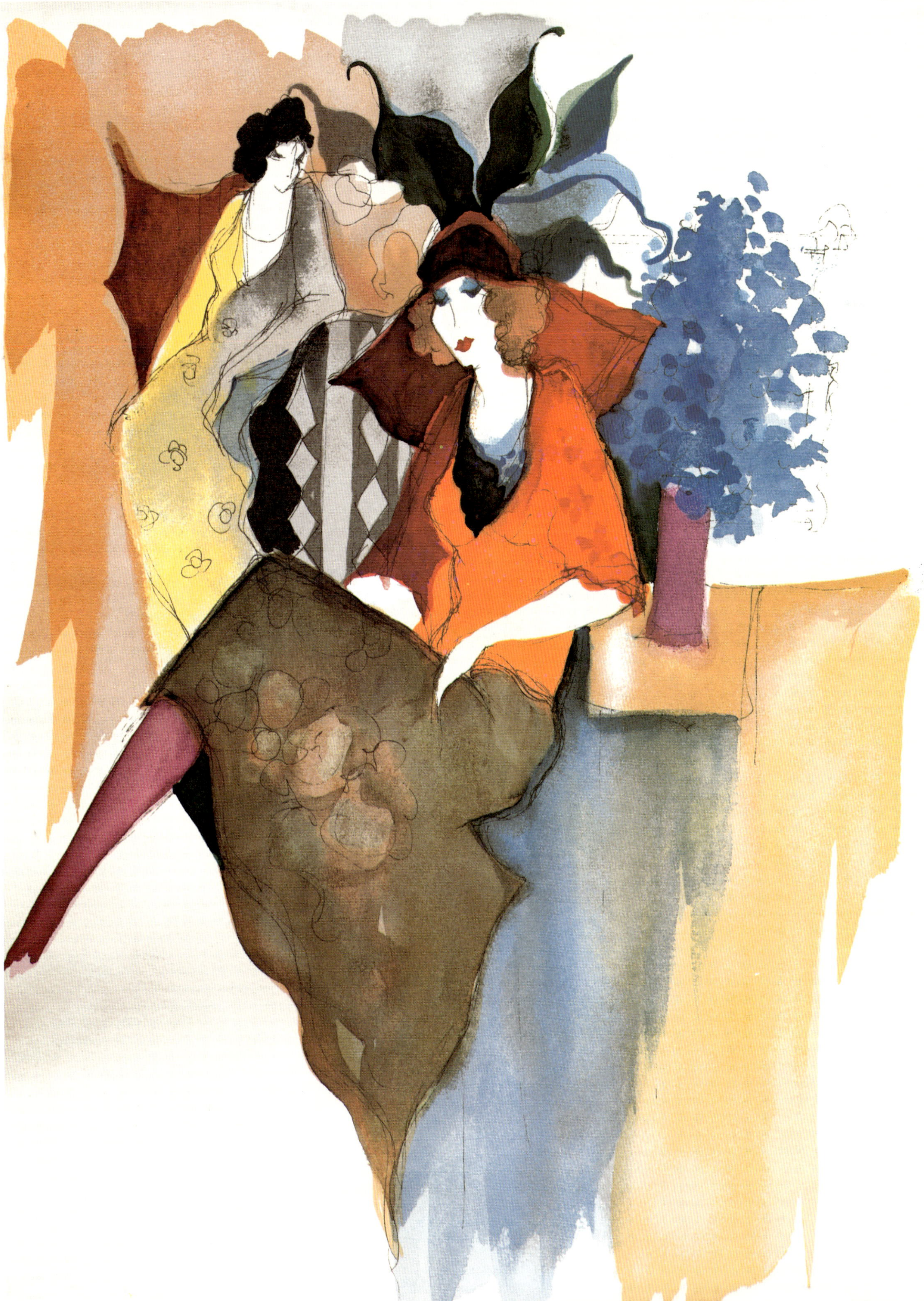

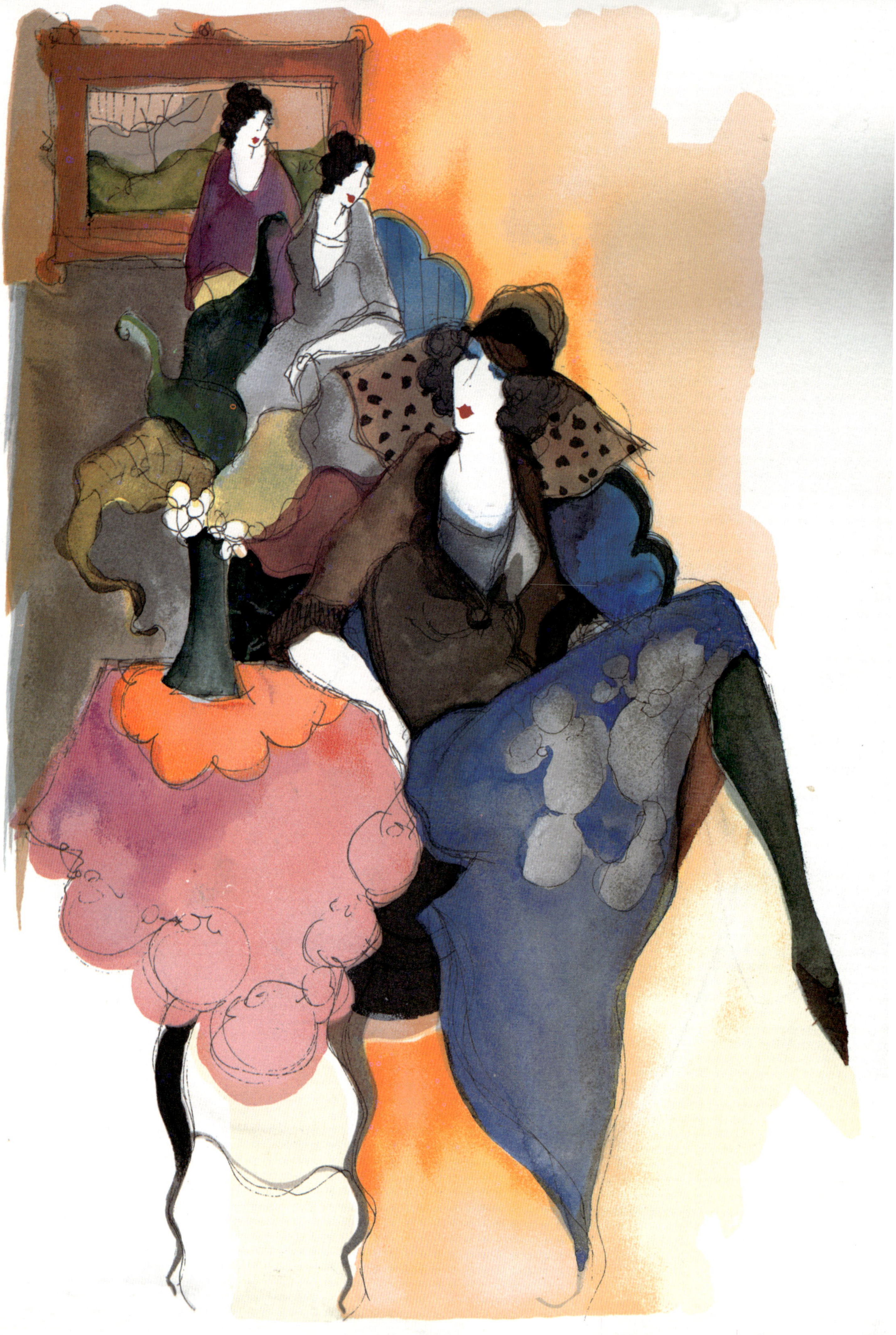

UNTITLED
11½" x 15¾"
Serigraph, Edition of 350

UNTITLED
11½" x 15¾"
Serigraph, Edition of 350

LE SALON III
16 ⅛" x 16 ⅛"
Serigraph, Edition of 350

LE SALON IV
16 ⅛" x 16 ⅛"
Serigraph, Edition of 350

LE SALON I
16 ⅛" x 16 ⅛"
Serigraph, Edition of 350

LE SALON II
16 ⅛" x 16 ⅛"
Serigraph, Edition of 350

MARA
9⅜" x 9½"
Serigraph, Edition of 350

UNTITLED
11½" x 15¾"
Serigraph, Edition of 350

153

SANDRA WITH FLOWERS
9⅜" x 9½"
Serigraph, Edition of 350

CATHERINE
13 5/8" x 11 1/2"
Serigraph, Edition of 350

UNTITLED
11½" x 15¾"
Serigraph, Edition of 350

157

ITZCHAK TARKAY
Selected One-Man Exhibitions

1983 – **Gemoart Gallery,** Tel Aviv, Israel

1984 – **Yad Lebanim,** Petach-Tikva, Israel

1985 – **Perry Art Gallery,** Tel Aviv Israel
Dugit Gallery, Tel Aviv, Israel

1986 – **Urek Gallery,** Israel

1987 – **The Windmill Gallery,** Israel
Gemoart Gallery, Tel Aviv, Israel
Weizman Gallery, Israel
Artexpo, New York, USA

1988 – **The Israel Experience Gallery,** Israel
Chetkin Gallery, New Jersey, USA
Ursus Press Gallery, Dusseldorf, Germany
Hatachana Gallery, Jerusalem, Israel

1989 – **Lorin Gallery,** New York, USA
Renejeau Gallery, Boston, USA
London Contemporary Art Gallery, London, UK
Gallery 454, Detroit, USA
Ursus Press Gallery, Dusseldorf, Germany

1990 – **Bruno Gallery,** Jerusalem, Israel
Dixon Bate Gallery, Manchester, UK
Lawrence Gallery, Santa Roa, USA
CCA Galleries, Oxford, UK
Ambassador Galleries, New York, USA
The Art Spectrum Gallery, Miami, USA
Perry Art Gallery, New York, USA
Various Exhibitions in Japan

ITZCHAK TARKAY
Selected One-Man Exhibitions

1991 – **Ambassador Galleries,** New York, USA
Tokyo Department Store Cultural Center, Japan
Perry Art Gallery, New York, USA
Bell Gallery, Belfast, Northern Ireland
Catto Gallery, London, UK
Renejeau Gallery, Boston, USA
World of Watercolors, London, UK
Park West Gallery, Detroit, USA

1992 – **Montpelier Gallery,** UK
Gallery D'Art, Paris, France
Gallery 2 Arcos, Spain
Lawrence Gallery, California, USA

1993 – **Barucci Gallery,** St. Louis, USA
Brewster Art Gallery, Pennsylvania, USA
Lake Falls Fine Arts, Maryland, USA

1994 – **Perry Art Gallery,** New York, USA
New Trends, Hong Kong
Seaton Gallery, Florida, USA
Davishire Interiors Gallery, Nashville, USA

1996 – **Artexpo,** New York, USA
Art Avenue Galleries, Cleveland, USA
Park West Gallery, Detroit, USA
Ambassador Gallery, New York, USA

1997 – **The Catto Gallery,** London, UK
Mensing Gallery, Hamm-Rhynern, Germany

CREDITS:
Layout and Design: Victor Forbes, Leonard Panar
Color Separations: Suzanne St. John
Production: Robert Olander
Printing: Enrique Robles
Design Consultation: John Russell
Photography Israel: Mehta Suchlowski
Photography USA: Paul Thacker
Project Coordinator: Richard Forbes
Archivist: Katherine Panar
Publishing Consultant: Jamie Ellin Forbes